O9-ABH-788

Twayne's United States Authors Series

Sylvia E. Bowman, *Editor*

INDIANA UNIVERSITY

David Graham Phillips

Courtesy of The New York Public Library

DAVID GRAHAM PHILLIPS

DAVID GRAHAM PHILLIPS

By ABE C. RAVITZ

Hiram College

CARNEGIE LIBRARY
LIVINGSTONE COLLEGE
SALISBURY, N. C. 28144

Twayne Publishers, Inc. :: New York

Copyright © 1966 by Twayne Publishers, Inc.

All Rights Reserved

Library of Congress Catalog Card Number: 66-12047

MANUFACTURED IN THE UNITED STATES OF AMERICA BY
UNITED PRINTING SERVICES, INC.
NEW HAVEN, CONNECTICUT

818.52
R256

To
LEE HAL

47248

DAVID GRAHAM PHILLIPS

by

ABE C. RAVITZ

David Graham Phillips, whose bold attack on the United States Senate evoked Teddy Roosevelt's famous "Man with a Muck-Rake" speech and thus introduced a new term into literary language, is here presented as a literary phenomenon of America's turbulent pre-World War I era of tabloid journalism. Led by a compelling ambition to become a responsible interpreter of American society, Phillips emerged from the world of the ephemeral dailies to create a body of work that suggests he be nominated prose laureate of the early twentieth century. His twenty-seven published volumes include *The Great God Success, The Conflict*, and the notorious *Susan Lenox; Her Rise and Fall*, a novel compared by many critics of the day to *The Scarlet Letter*.

This study is a thorough evaluation of Phillips' literary career. It sketches vividly the background and creative impetus of this once-famous name along publishers' row that has now faded into those very newspaper headlines of the past which he helped write and make.

Preface

WHEN David Graham Phillips died in 1911, America lost one of its most prolific authors of the pre-World War I period. A famous newspaperman of the time marked by yellow journalism, "scoops," "beats," and "exposés," Phillips moved into the area of serious free-lance writing; and, between the years 1901 and 1917, when his final posthumously published work appeared, he had produced enough volumes of fiction to suggest that he be nominated prose laureate of his era. Phillips' career has not been totally neglected, but nearly so. The subject of two unpublished doctoral dissertations of recent vintage and one rambling reminiscence of a biography brought out in 1932, David Graham Phillips remains identified today, however vaguely, as author of *Susan Lenox,* an early literary affront to the Society for the Suppression of Vice—or as perpetrator of "The Treason of the Senate," an exposé sponsored by William Randolph Hearst and damned by Theodore Roosevelt. Only a handful of articles attests to even a mild interest in the work of this novelist whose career epitomizes a type of American literary phenomenon which flourished briefly, yet prominently, during the turbulent epoch of muckraking and romance.

The purpose of this volume is to survey the life and work of Phillips, a once renowned and controversial author, and to evaluate his contribution to American letters of the so-called "strenuous age." The first two chapters present the formative influences on his life at home, as well as his years at college; his early newspaper experiences; and his first attempts at free-lance fiction. Chapters three and four analyze the early stages in Phillips' development as a novelist: his "frothy" romances, his aggressive arraignment of the plutocracy, and his fictional explorations into finance and politics. In chapter five his notorious *Cosmopolitan* series investigating the Senate is studied. The subsequent sections explore the major phase of Phillips' fiction, his scrutiny and dissection of the "New Woman": infidelity and divorce among the plutocrats; passion and parasitism among the *haut monde;* power and love in the lower depths. A summary conclusion endeavors to focus on a succinct perspective.

I wish to thank the Library of Congress, the Pennsylvania Historical Society, and the Princeton University Library for granting me access to the manuscript collections enumerated in the bibliographical section of this book. I am grateful also to Appleton-Century-Crofts and to Bobbs-Merrill, Phillips' publishers, for permission to quote from his writings. Special thanks are due Mrs. Albert J. Beveridge; the Hiram College Committee on Research; the staff of the Hiram College Library; assistants David Anderson and Virginia Franklin, and typist Michael Dunbar.

A. C. R.

Hiram, Ohio

Contents

Chronology

1867 David Graham Phillips born in Madison, Indiana, October 31.

1882 Matriculated at Asbury [DePauw] University, Greencastle, Indiana.

1885 Left Asbury and enrolled as a member of the junior class at Princeton.

1887 Graduated from Princeton; with the aid of college friends, secured the position of reporter for the Cincinnati *Times-Star*.

1888 Hired to the staff of rival Cincinnati *Commercial Gazette* as a feature writer and gossip columnist.

1890 Joined the staff of Charles A. Dana's nationally known New York *Sun*.

1891 Began to contribute essays and fiction to *Harper's Weekly*.

1893 Joseph Pulitzer hired Phillips as London correspondent for his famous New York *World*.

1896 Went to Europe as part of Pulitzer's entourage.

1897 Became an editorial writer for the *World*.

1901 Publication of first novel, *The Great God Success*, under the pseudonym "John Graham."

1902 Resigned from the *World* to devote himself to "serious" writing.

1903 First serialized novel, *Golden Fleece*, appeared in the *Saturday Evening Post*.

1903-
1904 *The Cost*, a novel exploring Wall Street fiscal and political machinations, serialized in the *Saturday Evening Post*.

1904-
1905 *The Plum Tree*, a work examining political corruption and its alliance with "lawless wealth," serialized in *Success*.

1905   *The Reign of Gilt,* a series of essays indicting the American plutocracy and attacking Thorstein Veblen published. Publication of *The Deluge,* a timely novel based on the eccentric career of Tom Lawson and "frenzied finance."

1906   "The Treason of the Senate," which aroused a storm of national controversy, serialized in William Randolph Hearst's *Cosmopolitan.*

1908   His drama *The Worth of a Woman* produced in New York. Publication of *Old Wives for New,* a study of American marriage.

1909   Publication of *The Hungry Heart,* a daring novel of marital infidelity.

1910   Publication of *The Husband's Story,* an examination of American success and divorce.

1911   David Graham Phillips died on January 24, murdered by an insane assassin.

1917   *Susan Lenox,* having been serialized in Hearst's *International Magazine* (1915-1917), was now published posthumously in two volumes.

David Graham Phillips

CHAPTER 1

The Gentleman from Indiana

ON THE AFTERNOON of Monday, January 23, 1911, David Graham Phillips left the Gramercy Park apartment he shared with his sister to pick up his mail at the nearby Princeton Club. He was a familiar figure both on Broadway and in the City's "back-yards," "a legend" on Park Row,[1] the street of New York tabloid journalism where he had learned the craft of the newsroom as well as the editorial office from Joseph Pulitzer himself. From an auspicious beginning as a reporter, Phillips had come to be regarded by many reputable critics as "the most distinguished American novelist of his time."[2] Only a few months earlier Benjamin O. Flower, influential editor of the *Arena* magazine, had asserted that "Mr. Phillips possesses all the elements essential to the creation of great and immortal fiction."[3] At the very moment he left the apartment for his walk to the Club, the prolific Phillips had been concluding the work on his galley proofs of *Susan Lenox: Her Fall and Rise;* four other completed manuscripts were in his desk. Indeed, he had once boasted, "If I were to die tomorrow, I would be six years ahead of the game."[4]

Outside the Princeton Club the novelist was accosted by Fitzhugh Coyle Goldsborough, a professional violinist obsessed with the conviction that Phillips' novels were little more than insidiously veiled attacks on the Goldsborough family of Washington, D.C. A paranoid who felt that Phillips was a literary "vampire" feasting on Goldsborough blood[5] and that his sister had been libelously portrayed in his anathema's most recent book, *The Fashionable Adventures of Joshua Craig,* the apparently insane violinist in his diary had characterized Phillips as a mortal aversion: "He is an enemy to society. He is my enemy."⁶ With the cunning one often notes in detective thrillers, Goldsborough had been very carefully shadowing the writer, studying his every move for days and, now, he stepped before the unsuspecting novelist and fired several shots directly at short range into his body. Turning the revolver on himself, the assassin committed suicide. David Graham Phillips lingered one day; he died the following evening at Bellevue Hospital shortly after eleven o'clock. Robert W. Chambers, a popular American novelist of the day, wrote, "... I cannot realize that he is dead, and often in the city streets—on Fifth Avenue in particular—I find myself glancing ahead for a glimpse of the tall, boyish, familiar figure.... His was a knightly mind; a paladin character."⁷ An esteemed critic, John Curtis Underwood, sadly lamented the passing of "the [Theodore] Roosevelt of American literature."⁸

I

The life and pulse of David Graham Phillips and his works seem inextricably attached to those glittering palaces of pre-World War I *haut monde* society of New York and to the shabby, predatory bucket-shops, Raines Law hotels, and dubious banking houses of lower Broadway. Although he came to represent the front-page glamor of metropolitan dailies and even to symbolize for a time the responsibility and integrity of the entire muckraking movement, Phillips was a small-town boy. The daring and sophisticated author who was to bellow "Treason!" at the United States Senate was born on October 31, 1867, at Madison, Indiana, a good distance from the centers of social and political intrigue that were to occupy his later studies in fiction and exposé. David Graham Phillips, Sr., was cashier of the National Branch Bank in Madison, an Ohio River town with a population in 1866 of ten thousand. Phillips' mother, Margaret Lee, "was a member of the family that included Light-Horse Harry Lee,"⁹ and her frank, decorous virtues Graham extolled by ascribing them to the admirable Mrs. Ellen Ranger in *The Second Generation,* who "had brought up her children in the old-fashioned way—her thoughts and usually her eyes, upon them all day, and one ear open all night."¹⁰ There were five children in the family: three older sisters, "Graham" and his younger brother.

Unlike conditions in the Dreiser family of Terre Haute, the circumstances here were comfortable and the family circle close. Yet, even during the boyhood of David Graham Phillips, roaming the several paved streets in Madison and watching with fascination the riverboats bound for Cincinnati, he was coming to observe the small-scale industrialization of his home town: "Here [were] four flouring mills, three iron foundries with machine shops, one brass foundry, several planing mills, and a dry-dock."[11] He was forever to retain a fondness for the uncomplicated economic structure that could circumscribe and satisfy a community of ten thousand; he was always repelled by monolithic corporate wealth and by the "grapple and grab" tactics of "bigness."[12]

Phillips, Sr., conducted early morning family prayers in the sitting room replete with "old-fashioned piano and bookcases";[13] and, while Graham would frequently find himself enthralled by "the story of Ezekiel or Enoch," the Bible did not completely satisfy the literary appetite of the banker's son. Before he was twelve, Phillips had "romped through Victor Hugo, Walter Scott, and Charles Dickens";[14] furthermore, in this early heyday of the dime novel,[15] the adventures of Seth Jones and the derring-do of Calamity Jane vied with Biblical heroes for his attention. Thus, this product of "Bible-reading Madison"[16] turned fifteen—a member of a seemingly uncomplicated Hoosier family such as one might encounter in the tales and chronicles of Meredith Nicholson. Pranks and jokes, declamation and recitation, public school and private tutor: "nothing unusual in Phillips's boyhood."[17]

Yet, there was. During this boyhood so free from biographical dilemma, David Graham Phillips and his sister Carolyn began a relationship of mutual devotion and love that lasted with a growing intensity until his death. A short time after Phillips had been killed, Anna S. Walling described the Graham–Carolyn relationship in these terms: "Again and again my mind dwelt on the magnitude of the love of this brother and sister, a love that glowed like a star, warmed like a sun. Every step of the way they took together. It was only a wonderful life that could create a love like that...."[18]

During their childhood in Madison came the first manifestations of the powerful feelings that were to draw these two so close together.[19] Carolyn once wrote: "Curious how distinctly I remember when Graham first fattened himself in my admiration. He could not have been more than eight. It was because he could keep a secret. He never told anything in all his life that anyone would wish him not to tell.... He never betrayed a confidence.... He was priest-like in this attitude. His understanding was sublime."[20]

Throughout most of his career (from 1894 on) David Graham Phillips, who remained a bachelor, lived under the same roof as his sister, first with Carolyn and her husband, Henry Frevert, whom she had married in 1880; then, after her separation, with Carolyn alone. In 1903 Phillips admitted in a letter: "I don't know what I should have done or whatever would become of me if it weren't for my sister."[21] Completely shattered at her brother's death, Carolyn, as his literary executrix, spent the last years of her own life preparing the publication of Phillips' posthumously released novels and lamenting with a passionate extravagance his sad passing.[22] The New York *World* remarked on the proclivity of Carolyn Phillips Frevert to "submerge her personality" in that of her brother.[23]

Carolyn, Graham's senior by six years, was able to observe his growing up with a patient and loving, almost maternal, regard. Thus it came about that even during the years in Madison this emotional, perceptive sister sensed the fundamental "inertia" (Phillips' word) that dominated the personality of her brother; she realized that he needed to be ignited and pushed to scale the ambitious heights she foresaw in his future. And the young adolescent himself, from his readings in Romantic fiction and sentimental dime novels, came to envision in his older sister the dream-like inspirational qualities he depicted in his first novel:

> He is coming home at one in the morning, worn out, sick at heart from the day's buffetings. As he puts his key into the latch, the door opens. There stands a handsome girl; her face is flushed; her eyes are bright; her lips are held up for him to kiss; she shows no trace of a day that began hours before his and has been a succession of exasperations and humiliations against which her sensitive nature, trained in the home of her father, a distinguished up-the-state Judge, gives her no protection.[24]

The image of Carolyn began early in his life to merge with his very own. Her role as inspiration, model, and confidante can hardly be overemphasized.

II

In 1882 Phillips, having graduated from Madison High School,[25] left his home town. His next station on the way to New York was Greencastle, Indiana, where this "fat, rosy-cheeked youngster"[26] matriculated at Asbury (DePauw) University to become the youngest member of the freshman class. His future profession he simply listed as "banking."[27]

Phillips, Sr., who had attended Asbury, felt confident that Graham would receive continued instruction in an atmosphere pervaded by the same fundamental piety that had characterized the household in Madison. In *The Cost* (1904), Phillips dealt with some of his Asbury academic backgrounds and attitudes and revealed that most of his fellow students were less inclined toward the Bible than toward pursuit of what Shelley had called "intellectual beauty," frequently sought in terms of the secular frontier:

> In theory and practice it was democratic, American, Western— an outgrowth of that pioneer life in which the men and the women had fought and toiled and enjoyed, side by side, in absolute equality, with absolute freedom of association. It recognized that its students had been brought up in the free, simple, frank way, that all came from a region where individualism was a religion, with self-reliance as the cardinal principle of faith and self-development as the goal.[28]

Phillips, a banker's son, seemed out of place:

> Most of Battle Field's youth came from the farms of that western country, the young men with bodies and brains that were strong but awkward. Almost all were working their way through. . . . They felt that life was a large, serious business impatiently waiting for them to come and attend to it in a large serious way better than it had ever been attended to before. They studied hard; they practiced oratory and debating. Their talk was of history and philosophy, religion and politics. They slept little; they thought—or tried to think—even more than they talked.[29]

One of these Asbury colleagues from the Middle West was at the moment in the very process of fabricating his own Horatio Alger success story, and it was to the everlasting good fortune of Phillips that this young scholar, Albert J. Beveridge—farmer, railroad hand, teamster, and "boy of the logging camp"—became his roommate. Beveridge had been admitted to Asbury partially on the basis of a letter he wrote to the president of the university: "I have been through . . . high school," the note read in part, "but I have no Latin and Greek. I have no money either. I mean by that, I have no money at all; but I feel that I must go to college."[30] Given his academic opportunity, Beveridge went on to represent Asbury in the State Oratorical Contest, "the supreme honor" at the school.[31]

Beveridge's compulsive sense of duty and routine began to impress the hitherto lethargic Phillips, who never attempted to conceal the lifelong admiration he entertained for "Bev"; indeed, in *The Cost* Phillips offered a glowing testimonial to his college roommate, characterizing Beveridge as Hampden Scarborough, political "demi-god": "He was standing pale and straight and mighty. He stretched out his hand, so large and strong, and somehow as honest as his eyes; the tempest stilled. . . . He staked all upon his voice; into it he poured all his energy, all his fire, all his white-hot passion for right and justice, all his scorn of the base and the low."[32]

For this "self-made man" Phillips always maintained a deep affection. In a frequent correspondence that lasted until the novelist's death, Beveridge was the first to welcome and praise his friend's latest publication, while Phillips is suspected of having influenced the liberal politics of the senator—an interesting reversal, the banker's son encouraging the progressivism of the logger.[33] The admiring Phillips had even gone so far as to characterize the restless idealism of Beveridge as akin to the chivalric tiltings of Don Quixote.[34] Like the Don, "Jeremiah" the insurgent was, symbolically, sent to political death the year Phillips was murdered.[35]

In college Phillips read much in history, economics, and philosophy. He went through Balzac and Zola and noted in the *Comédie Humaine* and the Rougon-Macquart cycle their plans to compose analytical, fictional studies of contemporary life on the broadest possible literary panorama. It was now, perhaps, that Phillips began to entertain his own nebulous thoughts of analyzing the fiber and of keeping the records of the American people. Yet it seems that Beveridge, rather than the French novelists, was the dominating influence on Phillips during his undergraduate days at Asbury. In conversation and debate these two flourished, though Phillips never issued a public challenge to his polished friend. It is evident, too, that the Beveridge philosophy was a good deal closer to Herbert Spencer than to the squire of La Mancha; for, in overcoming the economic handicaps of his early years, "Bev" had adopted as philosophical stance a thoroughly rugged pragmatism encompassing many of the Darwinist principles currently circulating throughout American intellectual circles. Beveridge was to articulate in print a short time later a firm statement of his muscular individualism:

> What hope does our complex civilization hold out to the children of hard circumstances? . . . Remember that every strong man who prevails in the merciless contest with events faces conditions which to weaker men seem inaccessible—are inaccessible. But it is the scaling of these heights, or the tunneling through them, or the blasting of them out of their way and out of existence, which makes these strong men strong. It is the overcoming of these obstacles day after day . . . which gives these mighty ones much of their power.[36]

At Asbury, Albert J. Beveridge lived this ethic in most successful terms; Phillips saw and learned the value of direction, dedication, and ambition. Work was soon to become a fetish with him, and Beveridge was to remain the total symbol of accomplishment. In an analysis of the prosperous temperament, Phillips, on the pages of *Success* magazine, cited the vibrant example of his college companion and generalized advice for those with "fire in their eyes and ginger in their feet":

> Hard work is the prime condition of achievement. Superiority consists in the possession of the combination of qualities—energy, tenacity, and intelligent plan—that make hard work bear a rich harvest. . . . Knock down the hard worker, and up he jumps to give battle more intelligently. Knock him down again; up he

jumps, more resolute than before.... The day is short, the task is heavy—and the only code ... is the high code of manly consideration and helpfulness for fellow workers. Idlers have their code; let them live among themselves and enjoy it.[37]

Thus, David Graham Phillips at Greencastle had been whirled into the orbit of Albert J. Beveridge and his living espousal of middle-border Darwinism; here was the vital sermon preached to Phillips at the small Methodist frontier college. When Beveridge graduated in 1885, a year ahead of his roommate, the gentleman from Madison decided it was time for him to move on too. Without taking a degree at Asbury, Phillips left to enroll as a junior at Princeton University. Yet much Hoosier residue would remain of his college experience; and much learning not described in the Asbury catalogue had come to him from his ideal of success: "Bev."

III

The strain of piety that had by this time become very familiar to David Graham Phillips through educative exposure at home and to some degree at school was now to be intensified during his stay at Princeton. Then in the final years of the administration of President James McCosh, noted psychologist, philosopher, and licensed "preacher of the Established Church of Scotland,"[38] the College of New Jersey in outlining the program for juniors included among its required courses the Bible and Greek, along with physics, mathematics, history, and English.[39] Phillips was a major in Arts; and, while his career plans still remained vague, he found himself in an intellectual maelstrom that can be personified best by the feverish scholarly activity of Dr. McCosh himself, as well as by the impact of Scotch Realism which had already infiltrated the Princeton intellectual tradition. Thus the metaphysical atmosphere surrounding Phillips circumscribed an ethic of Scotch "common sense" philosophy, the scheme of thinking that was "forthright, down-to-earth, rational, and yet pious,"[40] a challenging inquiry "enlightened, yet conservative:

The Scots and their American interpreters acknowledged that men make mistakes, but they attributed these not to failures in the mechanism of human understanding but to errors of association and inference; they were marks of original sin, and were to be overcome by the combined help of divine grace and of study and education. The realists were not anti-intellectuals, but they had no use for the extravagances of Emerson and Bronson Alcott.[41]

McCosh was, perhaps, the last titan of this "school," and his mark on Princeton even before Phillips' brief residence there had been indelibly impressed. His books on divine government, realistic philosophy, the emotions, and discursive thought reveal more than casual investigations into the contemporary desideratum of science versus religion; the good doctor was concerned with what Spencer called "first principles." McCosh once wrote, "In my first published work, 'The Method of Divine Government,' I sought to unfold the plan by which God governs the world, and I found it to be in an orderly manner...." He felt, intuitively, that truth was his: "I am pleased to discover that intelligent Christians are coming round gradually to the views which I have had the courage to publish."[42]

Inevitably this dilemma aroused by Darwin and Evolution came frequently to the attention of Dr. McCosh, and in the manner of Scotch Realism he sensibly sought to achieve the logical reconciliation of the worlds belonging to spirit and matter: "I do not propose ... to prove anew the existence of God.... My aim rather is to show that the doctrine of evolution does not undermine the argument from Final Cause, but rather strengthens it by furnishing new illustrations of the wisdom and goodness of God."[43]

The *Nassau Literary Magazine* reviewed with enthusiasm McCosh's work on Herbert Spencer "because it appears as if Mr. Spencer would take a firm hold on America ..."[44] and undermine, perhaps, the faith of susceptible undergraduates. The students, nearly all of whom came to know Dr. McCosh personally (there were only eighty-six members of Phillips' class), were enthusiastic about the clarity of his vision, the brilliance of his mind, and the ruggedness of his speech.[45]

Again Phillips was confronted by an admirable example of work and dedication, of immersion in the problems of life and thought. Indeed, Graham's own interest at Princeton in communicating his reflections on various aspects of life—too mean, one suspects, for McCosh to notice, like Woman Suffrage—soon won for him the nickname of La Bouche.[46] Some of the ideas so frequently tossed about the room of "Louis Phillipe" late at night, however, were apparently finding their way onto paper. Whether influenced by McCosh's prodigious output or by suggestion from classmates, Phillips began to exhibit the "literary bent" that made him "known in college."[47]

One has only the testimony of members of the Class of '87 to substantiate the claim that Phillips had now begun to write fiction, for the *Nassau Literary Magazine* published none of his efforts; nor did the college newspaper carry any of his literary productions. Evidence in the form of an enigmatic statement issued by his classmates seems to point to the fact that his work was uniformly rejected by college editors: "... he had written things for the university paper and had tried out a few of the magazines that didn't care for his stories."[48]

It is possible that at this time Phillips was aligned with several academic malcontents, also interested in writing, who set up a mild clamor for academic attention to be focused on the new discipline of journalism. One James Paige stated the problem in the *Nassau Literary Magazine:* "We have schools of law, of medicine, of divinity; our colleges offer electives which bear directly on these professions, but who ever heard of a school of journalism[?]"[49] Perhaps Phillips was giving a retrospective summary of his position and status at Princeton as he recorded the opening job interview of Howard, hero of *The Great God Success:*

"On your college paper, I suppose?"
"No, I never wrote even a letter to the editor."
"Took prizes for essays?"
"No, I never wrote if I could help it."
"But you like to write?"
"I'd like to learn to write."[50]

The interest in journalism could have been instigated by friendship with fellow students Clarence and Marshall Halstead, whose father was then editor of the Cincinnati *Commercial-Gazette,* or perhaps by a sudden desire to see his ideas in print, to present issues beyond the confines of his dormitory room.

That President McCosh succeeded in orienting Phillips some-what toward speculations upon Darwinism and its current influence on the status of God and Man will be borne out by analysis of his novels and thought. That the good doctor failed in one area of this Hoosier's undergraduate education is testified by the fact that Phillips was one of only five in the entire Class of '87 who gave "None" as answer when asked for his religious denomination; his politics were safely Republican, and in the vast majority.[51] Always lying in literary ambush for any mani-festation of hypocrisy, Phillips later came to regard piety as the most prevalent subterfuge of his day for political malfeasance and economic plundering. Certainly it would have been social suicide to publicize with antipathy his complete revolt from Bible-reading mornings at home, Asbury, and Princeton; but the fact that Phillips let his feelings be known might have caused his quiet, subtle alienation from the mainstream of campus literary life. Or, perhaps there was a self-imposed isolation from the literary clique as a kind of intellectual discipline.

He never was part of the creative coterie at Princeton, but it was at this time that Phillips made the acquaintance of an anonymous novelist, later revealed as George Gissing, whose *Demos: A Story of English Socialism* appeared in 1886. The novel became the subject "for exhaustive review"[52] by Phillips, and it can make clear the political prejudices and artistic pre-dilections he developed at and carried from Princeton. *Demos* was to furnish him with a store of literary types and materials.

Briefly, the Gissing novel, rushed into print to make literary capital of the notorious proletarian riots in Trafalgar Square,[53] deals with the rise, fall, and death of Richard Mutimer, a Socialist laborer who through a legal freak inherits a huge estate. With the best of intentions he transforms Wanley into New Wanley, a workingman's paradise community. As leader of this revolutionary movement, Mutimer comes to be regarded as a philanthropist; he is named "Man of the Day" in the London *Chronicle;* but he begins to suffer "from the *malaise* peculiar to men who suddenly acquire riches."[54] Forsaking his faithful sweetheart of the slums, Mutimer marries a "lady"; he begins to have *paté de foie gras* for breakfast; he comes to distrust the coarse brute Demos, the very source of his power and popularity. Through yet another freak circumstance, the fortune is lost and Mutimer must return to the lower depths; but, spoiled by his days of gentility, he drifts on the fringes of Socialism until he becomes a private banker ("It's a trick the capitalists found out. Interest was a good discovery, but compound interest a good deal better"). He fails in this enterprise and is finally stoned to death by rioters inflamed at the thought that Mutimer deserted his class and his principles. Comrade Roodhouse takes over; he is no "namby-pamby Socialist ... such as the late Dukeling of New Wanley." Mutimer had been made by aroused Demos, and there is more than a mere inkling of tragedy in his ultimate realization of futility and failure: "Listen to them! That's the People, that is! I deserve killing, fool that I am, if only for the lying good I've said of them."[55]

The Reverend Wyvern appears in a kind of choric role, as almost a direct counterpart to Mutimer. He has no faith in radicalism; nor does he sympathize with the wealthy: "I am with the Socialists, in that I denounce the commercial class, the bourgeois, the capitalists ... as the supremely maleficent." Wyvern goes on to excoriate the commercial wealthy in terms that were most impressive to David Graham Phillips: "They hold us at their mercy and their mercy is nought. Monstrously hypocritical, they cry for progress when they mean increased opportunities of swelling their own purses at the expense of those they employ, and of those they serve; vulgar to the core, they exalt a gross idea of well-being, and stink in their prosperity. The very poor and the uncommercial wealthy alike suffer from them; the intellect of the country is poisoned by their influence."[56]

The antithesis of democratic are Wyvern's views on "universal education" and its unfortunate results:

Its results affect all classes, and all for the worse. I said that I used to have a very bleeding of the heart for the half-clothed and quarter-fed hangers-on to civilisation; I think far less of them now than of another class in appearance much better off. It is a class created by the mania of education, and it consists of those unhappy men and women whom unspeakable cruelty endows with intellectual needs whilst refusing them the sustenance they are taught to crave. Another generation, and this class will be terribly extended, its existence blighting the whole social state.[57]

The sympathies of the Reverend Wyvern remain polarized: the destitute and the opulent are joined in a brotherhood of grief: "The life of the very poorest is a struggle to support their bodies; the richest ... are overwhelmed with such a mass of artificial troubles that their few moments of genuine repose do not exceed those vouchsafed to their antipodes." He has come to regard with sadness "the misery of the rich under the scourge of their own excesses."[58]

Nearly twenty years after Gissing had written these sentiments, Phillips described for readers of the *Saturday Evening Post* some of "The Penalties of Plutocracy": "The supreme penalty of poverty is the associations it imposes; and that is also the supreme calamity of wealth. Poverty's associations breed one set of moral degradations; wealth's associations breed another set. ... The plutocrat ... is to be pitied. His soul is ravaged by a disease, as truly a disease as the morphine or drink habit. And it gives him no rest until it thrusts him into his grave—and it ravages his heirs unto the third and fourth generations."[59] As the mother of Richard Mutimer cried, "It's my belief as money's the curse of this world; I never knew a trouble yet as didn't somehow come of it, either 'cause there was too little or else too much."[60]

But, long before Phillips took up writing as a professional, Gissing's Reverend Wyvern had begun to prompt him. The vicar had made a general observation about a contemporary phase of European radicalism: "But English Socialism! It is infused with the spirit of shopkeeping; it appeals to the vulgarest minds; it keeps one eye on personal safety, the other on the capitalist's strong-box; it is stamped commonplace, like everything originating with the English lower classes."[61] Phillips quoted Wyvern's exact words (he was later to appropriate Veblen) in his Princeton report when evaluating an aspect of British radicalism: "English Socialism is a peculiar type. It is the natural offspring of the English mind. It is more sordid, more openly brutal, than any other. It is infused with the spirit of the shopkeeper. It appeals to the vulgarest minds. It keeps one eye on personal safety and the other on the capitalist's strong-box."[62] Phillips went on to arraign the renegade Mutimer as "a type" who "betrays" his former friends and associates in the labor movement: "Is not this the natural result? It was inevitable. . . ."

For Wyvern, however, Phillips reserves his heartiest agreement and endorses with spirit the major views of the articulate clergymen: "Education brings unsatisfied and insatiable longings that ignorance never knows. Say what you will, increase education and you increase pain. But his [Wyvern's] renunciation of the bourgeois is most praiseworthy. This indeed is the worst class of modern society. The hypocrisy of their cry of progress is well shown up."[63]

The tones of a genteel conservatism are sounded here, early in the career of David Graham Phillips. Like James Fenimore Cooper, Phillips mistakenly regarded himself as a subscriber to the tenets of American democracy, when in reality a benevolent autocracy, preferably of the intellect, would have been most amenable to his personality. Despite later research expeditions into the tenements of New York and the cesspools of metropolitan vice, he was a banker's son from Princeton. Phillips was to dramatize in his novels, however, the thesis that the power élite could be effectively bought or blatantly stolen by the political brigand rather than earned by the impractical intellectual. On the other hand, like Gissing in his proletarian novel, Phillips regarded the people as a great "beast."

But there was more in *Demos* for Phillips than a fictional excoriation of British Socialism. Aside from the most prominent themes—hypocrisy, arrogance, greed—on which the mechanics of the plot depend, Gissing interlaced through his novel a Victorian sentiment to unify his portraits of disillusionment, poverty, and death. Politics became a force that necessarily dehumanized the individual; it was a vast game that decimated all that was fragile and valuable to Eldon, Mutimer's successor as master: "From my point of view no movement can be tolerated which begins with devastating the earth's surface. You will clothe your workpeople better, you will give them better food and more leisure; in doing so you injure the class that has finer sensibilities, and give power to the class which not only postpones everything to material wellbeing, but more and more regards intellectual refinement as an obstacle in the way of progress."[64]

The presentation of an incompatible marriage stems from

these sentiments as Mutimer, the commoner with unreasonable ambitions ("I say...how would it sound," [he cries] "Richard Mutimer, First President of the English Republic?"), and his wife Adela, a fashionable gentlewoman, have no basis for communication: "Did he love her? She had never asked him that, and all at once she felt a longing to hasten after him and utter the question. Would he know what she meant?"[65] The profligate brother, the slighted fiancée, the death via broken heart, and the license of great wealth further comprise the total material poured into *Demos,* all borne with a Victorian equanimity loosely hinged on the simple plot. An epigrammatic wisdom is sprinkled through the novel too: "When women are educated, they will take the world as it is, and decline to live on illusions"; "Gentleman... is the vulgarest of denominations!... A man's a man, I take it, and what need is there to lengthen the name?"; "Two vices are growing among us to dread proportions—indifference and hatred; the one will let poverty languish at its door, the other will hound on the vassal against his lord."[66] And side by side with the scenes of economic depravity, with the flashes of incisive persiflage, are the aromas and perfumes of sentimental romance that Phillips frequently came to adopt: "The wild rose of her cheeks made rivalry for an instant with the richer garden blooms, and the subsiding warmth left a pearly translucency as of a lily petal against the light. She held her hand to him, delicately gloved, warm...."[67]

Demos, in short, can be regarded as a literary compendium for Phillips whose logical picture of the universe was intensified by the Realism of Dr. McCosh in matters philosophical and whose cosmic vision now continued in the orbit of Beveridge and Gissing: a practical and pragmatic perception of man as a unidimensional being able to control his passions by will and to channel his drives into productive, socially desirable avenues. Gissing showed also that man need not prevail, however: his lack of refinement and his failure to perceive love or respond to natural beauty can bring about his defeat.

The universe David Graham Phillips entered as he left Princeton was for him a utilitarian world—one of facts, figures, and proofs. He had not yet found a place in it, nor had he decided upon the course of his career. He would go to Cincin-

nati, not too far upriver from Madison, and with advance notices
from the Halstead brothers to their father try his hand at
crashing the glamorous field of journalism. Louis Phillipe La
Bouche was to begin his researches into peripheral humanity as
the first step in what gradually developed into an obsessive
ambition; to become recording secretary of the American people.

CHAPTER 2

The Metropolis

NOTHING IN THE BACKGROUND of David Graham Phillips could have augured the unbelievable success that immediately came to him as a newspaper reporter in Cincinnati. His postgraduate education took the form of an adventure in journalism, a career luckily thrown open to him through the friendships made at Princeton; and after just a few days with the *Times-Star*, Phillips "covered himself with glory."[1] Whether Graham's vigorous drive for success as a reporter came from the encouragement of his sister Carolyn or from his own desperate need to emulate at last the "self-made" principles articulated by Beveridge, the young reporter immersed himself completely in the newspaper world "brilliantly yet laboriously."[2] Soon raised to twenty-five dollars a week, he was hired away by the rival *Commercial-Gazette* for forty; and he continued there as a sensation of Buckeye journalism. From 1887 to 1890 Phillips went about learning his craft, developing a pair of "keen eyes" and sharpening an "analytical mind" to guide the aggressive "reporter's trained hand."[3] An admirer later observed that, like Dickens, Phillips came to know the "world like a book."[4]

Phillips circulated freely throughout local society as both observer and participant: "He was secure in his position as star reporter of the town. He was absorbed in what he was doing. He went from fire to murder; from suicide to political sensation. He talked with policeman, fireman, criminal, cab-driver, actor, politician, capitalist. . . ."[5] Phillips once confided to Bailey Millard, editor of *Cosmopolitan*: "I have . . . avoided riding in a carriage or an auto, for I know that the man or woman who does it gets out of sympathy with the masses."[6]

He came to see firsthand the various operations of city life, its poverty and its politics, its vitality and its trivia. Journalism soon "became his passion" and he developed a glib flair for the timely and the "human interest." On special assignments he wrote essays on beer mugs, bread, rouge, socialism, and handshaking. He conducted the "Notes About Town" column ("A bank is a great place for taking cold—so many drafts passing through all the time")[7]—a forerunner of the Poor Richard Junior "snappy" paragraphs that George Horace Lorimer, Graham's literary patron and discoverer, was about to initiate in the *Saturday Evening Post*.

In short, the twenty-three-year-old Phillips quickly ran the gamut of experience on the provincial newspapers, and—with Carolyn to oversee his work, to collect a painstaking scrapbook of his contributions, and to prod his indolent tendencies, as journalese of the day would have it—Phillips' inflamed ambition finally urged him to storm the citadels of metropolitan dailies on Park Row in New York. In May, 1890, Phillips at a salary of fifteen dollars a week was hired to the reportorial staff of the New York *Sun*, a world-famous paper owned and published by Charles A. Dana. On April 11, 1891, David Graham Phillips, Sr., wrote the following in a letter to Albert J. Beveridge, Indianapolis attorney-at-law: "I am glad you take such an interest in my son Graham. . . . I had a letter last evening from him; he is well and doing well. . . . He wrote me when he first went to New York and used these words: 'Here I am in this great city, and no man, woman, or child cares whether I am dead or alive; but I will make them care before I am done with them.' "[8]

I *Toward Fiction*

The chronicle of Phillips' success with the *Sun* bears remarkable similarity to the fictional achievement in the newspaper world of Howard, hero of *The Great God Success* (1901). Like his character creation, David Graham Phillips had, through his apprenticeship covering news events ranging from night court to ecclesiastical council, evolved his own philosophy of journalism, a call which demanded "the sharpening of all the faculties; the service of truth and right and human betterment, in daily combat with injustice and error and falsehood; the arousing and stimulating of the drowsy minds of the masses of mankind. . . ."[9] He came to infuse his stories with an "atmosphere of sincerity, of realism, the marks of an acute observer, without prejudice and with a justifiable leaning toward a belief in the fundamental worth of humanity."[10] It is also true that both Howard and Phillips became "stars" by their sentimental coverage of the same "Lost Baby Found" story, for the journalist-turned-novelist appropriated liberally from his own newspaper tale in recasting the scenes reported by his young, ambitious literary counterpart. Promoted to space-assignment at which he might earn seventy or eighty dollars a week, Phillips soon became "a seasoned *Sun* man."[11]

Accustomed to quick, satisfying recognition, he felt ready to expand the area of his creative activity; and by early 1891 Phillips had begun to orient himself toward some apparent literary possibilities of the "news" he was covering, to think in terms of fusing his experience in journalism with that of art. Some of his human-interest observations and tales somewhat beyond the category of news stories began to appear in *Harper's Weekly*. Like many another metropolitan reporter in *fin de siècle* America, Phillips began to dabble in what fellow journeymen reporters called "outside writing." And, with the greater thematic freedom tolerated and even encouraged by the current periodicals, sprouts of the enthusiastic reporter's philosophy began to peep through his early contributions to *Harper's*.

Phillips recorded with more irony than nostalgia the passing of the glamorous legend surrounding the American Indian in "The Sioux Chiefs Before the Secretary," an essay featuring a rather tawdry picture of former noble savages—knights of the prairies:

> They were in an office in the midst of civilization. . . . They were not in buckskin, not gayly bedecked with feathers. They wore cheap, ill-fitting store clothes, white shirts, old-fashioned collars, curious neckties. . . . The time was when Indian chiefs, scornful and supercilious, stalked into the council-chambers of the whites and demanded their rights, and more perhaps. That was not so long ago. But see now to what these kinsmen of Philip and Tecumseh are come . . . the boldness, the courage, the spirit were gone with the paint and the feathers, the leggins and the moccasin.

They plead for the chance to become civilized. The warpath shall be no more. The tomahawk . . . the warwhoop, the cautious trail over the track-less prairie—all are out of date, as traditional as Cooper's Mohicans. The council fire is exchanged for the steam radiator of a government office. The Indian affects cigars, and buys clothes from Baxter Street. . . . Sitting Bull died none too soon.[12]

The humbling of once mighty chiefs by civilization, the transience of regality and the vulgar trappings of contemporary society as juxtaposed with the royal folklore of yesteryear were emphasized by Phillips, who even at this stage of his writing began to develop a focus on those unfortunates scrambling about the bottom rung of the social ladder in New York. The Bowery derelicts who at the time were beginning to interest Stephen Crane and the slum ghettos that were captivating the readers of Bruno Lessing,[13] Graham's colleague on the *Sun*, also caught the attention of Phillips. From the Indian and his loss of dignity and selfhood, the author turned in "The Union of Sixth Avenue and Broadway" to a scrutiny of the topic that was to remain an intrinsic part of his deepest literary interest throughout his entire career, the American Woman—her status and her struggles in an essentially hostile environment:

In the streets are the colored lamps of the cars, the yellow eyes of carriages; and as the docked and spirited horses pass, you see faintly through the rain-dashed windows women in handsome evening bravery. Their eyes shine out from gauze-like head coverings. There is something surpassingly attractive about the sight of a woman in evening dress in a closed carriage on a dreary, rainy night. . . . Here live chorus girls and second-rate actresses. . . . These girls have short curly hair generally, and bright, keen eyes and ready tongues. They range all the way in both directions from doubtful respectability; they are self-reliant and man-like in many ways; they have learned not to be bashful in asking things of an inattentive world. To be rid of the shop or the factory, and to live in their own flat, is their dream; loss of youth and poverty is their horror. Sometimes they realize the dream; the horror they never miss. . . .[14]

One begins to see, too, the paradox surrounding Phillips' interest in and involvement with the materials he felt would rescue him from editorial room and city desk. The headline, the quick attraction, the story: here were Phillips' fundamental concerns, all strongly attached to journalism, the discipline he never escaped. His desire was to sketch for immediate recognition and straightaway, at-sight communication; a major hazard of so mediocre an aim, however, is constant neglect, as the "timely" story often fades into an insignificant footnote to social history. A detailed character analysis, for example, that would differentiate the personal and psychic problem of one second-rate actress from another held no trenchant interest for Phillips even in 1891. His prose experiments now transformed him into a journalist expanding his reach, a would-be artist in search of material, but employing familiar serviceable expedients which he tracked down as methodically and as relentlessly as he pursued a story lead for the *Sun*.

One senses the vague pieces of a full-length story in Phillips' treatment of "The City's Back Yard": "In one of these heaps there was [*sic*] a broken cradle, a hobby-horse with the tail and the name and the legs off, a chromo of the Virgin with a hole knocked in it, a worked motto 'God Bless our Home.' . . . A rat gnawed the frame of the motto, and one morning the foreman found the 'God Bless' eaten out. So for a month or more 'our Home' surmounted the little heap of rags and ruins."[15] The author has presented a rather melodramatic symbol, but he has left the internal drama of the tale unwritten, hovering in the nebulous world of his limited vision. Phillips' most frequent contributions to *Harper's Weekly* continued to reveal his talent as one chained closely to the newsroom desk; the mechanics and periphery of journalism still commanded his allegiance. The merely piquant melodramas of irony, of sentiment, and of romance were the major total effects he strove to create.

On May 23, 1891, *Harper's Weekly* published Phillips' story of domestic tension and rivalry, "The First-Born," a valuable document in charting the historical development of the novelist, for the tale deals with a conflict that Phillips would return to again and again throughout his career in fiction: the psychological pressures of marriage and the sudden, seemingly capricious disintegration of love.[16] In this "short, short story" Phillips endeavored to chart the subtle shift of passion in a woman whose enthusiastic and wholehearted dedication to loving motherhood has succeeded in alienating her rejected husband:

At first he was awed by the change in her face, by the mysterious being whose head nestled to her shoulder, by the wonder of birth and maternity. Then, as the meaning of it for him came to his mind, the instant thought was that she was more lost to him than if she were dead. A few days before, her eyes had in them the sparkle and the frequent flash of passionate love for him. . . . Her face now shone with the calmness and serenity of a mother. And the sad conviction came to the husband that the change was final. . . . He arose and stood looking bitterly out of the window.[17]

Both the theme and Phillips' treatment of it are characteristic of the method he began to develop during the *Sun* years. His people are scarcely alive as individuals; they are stalking symbols of individual conflicts and social symptoms the author was beginning to analyze under his microscope. While there exists in this early writing an overpowering sense of the ephemeral, and while the scrupulous detailing that Phillips incorporated into the sketches have little purpose beyond the descriptive, the literary malaise forever to afflict his prose was now painfully evident: there was little conscious experimentation in his fiction.

He was, nevertheless, working furiously. A sense of duty, if not of destiny, seemed to possess him; and his reportorial roving eye now began to wander expectantly toward the golden dome of the Pulitzer Building on Park Row. In 1893 Phillips left Dana and the *Sun* after three years of labor that moulded in great part all the novelist would ever become. He next moved to the last stop in his journalistic peregrinations: a post on the New York *World*, a high-pressure, reformist sheet run by the iron-fisted Joseph Pulitzer, "liberator of journalism."[18]

The final phase of Phillips' education now began. Several years before Phillips joined the staff, Pulitzer had published in an editorial this statement of principle:

There is the aristocracy of Central Park. The low Victoria, adapted to exhibit boots, stockings, and skirts as freely as hats and shoulder wraps. The sleigh with more nodding plumes than would deck out a company of lancers. There is the sordid aristocracy of the ambitious matchmakers, who are ready to sell their daughters for barren titles to worthless foreign paupers. . . . The new *World* believes that such an aristocracy ought to have no place in the republic—that the word ought to be expunged from the American vocabulary.[19]

Phillips, too, soon began to scathe the American aristocrats "and their imitators and followers, all palpitating with eagerness to be 'cultured like the high folks over yonder.' "[20]

II *Pulitzer and Russell*

"ACCURACY—TERSENESS—ACCURACY"[21] was the message Joseph Pulitzer imparted to staff members of the *World*, and the change in tenor and atmosphere Phillips experienced in the move from *Sun* to *World* must have been truly startling for him. Pulitzer ran his paper as a general would command a combat army. He collected an "entourage" of well-paid "experts" who became his personal consultants on various realms of current interest and who marshaled all editorial force against the antagonist of the moment in whatever current Pulitzer crusade was then hanging fire, whether it be "boodle" aldermen, "privileged corporations," or even William Randolph Hearst, the publisher later to employ Phillips' talents with the muck rake.

While working for Pulitzer, Phillips was subjected to a series of journalistic experiences incalculable in scope: from London correspondent "on perpetual assignment"[22] to "keyhole" reporter; from contributor to "Stories of the Day" to explorer of New York's municipal scene; and from covering fashionable social events to reporting on snowstorms. Pulitzer waxed hot and cold, however, about Phillips and his qualifications, for the dynamic little publisher doubtless felt that his "steal" from the *Sun* had become a spoiled prima donna. And David Graham Phillips, who in the heat of combat atmosphere generated in the *World* was unable to contribute to "outside" periodicals, felt that his talents were misused and his skill exploited in a hopelessly pedestrian manner. Yet by 1896 Phillips had become Pulitzer's "expert" on "European politics"; and, by 1898, he was contributing very heavily to the *World* editorial page. The initials "D.G.P.," furthermore, were seen under many an office-rigged "Letter to the Editor."[23] He was dispatched occasionally to swing about the country on especial assignment, but behind every dispatch, report, or policy was Pulitzer; Phillips was not permitted to forget that he was but a workaday hack, performing as ordered by his superior.

A letter from Pulitzer to Phillips reveals how closely the "general" was surveying his puppet army of reporters and orienting specifically both their writings and points of view: "You may also write a short dispatch from Cleveland about the outlook in Ohio, trying to treat McLean as kindly as possible. Don't lie for him . . . but pass over things you would feel like saying against him for personal as well as political reasons. . . . I want you to write up Bryan at home. . . . I want you to be kind to him, tell all the truth possible, strictly and exactly, but from a kindly rather than antipathetic point of view."[24] Thus, to study the pages of the *World* is to encounter mainly the total and complete personality of Joseph Pulitzer in all its dominating force. Of Phillips' sentiments in their variety of shadings and depths at the time of his association with the *World*, we can, therefore, be somewhat dubious. But Pulitzer's brand of journalism had genuine attraction for him: the exposé of criminal vice, the war on civic corruption, the constant social crusades against disease and poverty—what Jacob A. Riis called "the many headed dragons hard to slay."[25]

All of these frontal conflicts of men in action revealed for Phillips the basic tensions he would try to purvey in his fiction. The *World*, "leading Democratic journal of the country,"[26] was a new educational mill; and it was, again, the type which Phillips, with a vicious contempt for formal schooling, appreciated; here was not to be found "an ignorant professor . . . of some university where little of value is taught or learned."[27] As a *World* staff member, also, Phillips, in addition to knowing at first hand the king of the golden dome, became associated with Charles Edward Russell, editor and Socialist: "A close friendship developed [and] they were inseparable companions."[28] Indeed, these two newspapermen thought much alike. Claimed Russell, seven years Phillips' senior, and an opponent of "collegiate" learning, ". . . the only education I ever had that amounted to anything was when I was a police reporter on the East Side of New York."[29] When in 1906 the New York *Truth-Seeker* enumerated a list of men "with the muck rake," Russell and his young colleague were introduced side by side.[30] The relationship meant much to Phillips.

When Charles Edward Russell officially made application for admission into the Socialist Party, the event was celebrated by newspaper headlines.[31] Aside from his experience as an editor for Pulitzer, Russell had become the notorious "corruption-

hunter" of *Everybody's Magazine,* as well as the passionate
opponent of America's Beef Trust: "Russell lays bare the beef
roast rare / And carves the butcher man."[32] Russell left the
World in 1897, but for two years he helped identify for Phillips
those impediments of life extending beyond the facile interest of
the rotogravure; for this incendiary Socialist felt an affinity for
and a commitment to the so-called Types from the City Streets
as well as a righteous antipathy toward The Powers that Prey:
"You see," he cried, "the vast and senseless accumulation of the
few, and the multiplied and manifold sufferings of the many."[33]
Russell, who eventually published three volumes of poetry, once
composed "A Little Song for 'The System'":

> Wanton and waste and wallow,
>   Stretch out your easeful span.
> Bemock with pretense hollow
>   The laboring soul of man.
>
> . . . .
>
> Debauch, debase, bemire;
>   Load the altars with loathesome dust;
> Quench the old sacred fire,
>   Give over to greed and lust.
>
> . . . .
>
> Rot out the heart of the nation,
>   Control its courts and camps
> Thrust into the highest station,
>   Your smooth, smug thieves and scamps.[34]

A stroll by Russell on the lower East Side did not inspire a
dialect verse of the ghetto and its comical immigrant types, but
"Essex Street: A Bourgeois Excursion":

> I note gaunt cheeks and wolfish eyes
>   Bare children with ill-covered bones,
> And hear what awful hymnals rise
>   Of mocking moans.
>
> . . . .
>
> How lean and leaden looks the face
>   Above the flying needle bent!
> I wonder from what alien race
>   That wolf was sent
> To plague us with its hungry jaws....[35]

One can feel, as Russell noted, that these "spectres" literally robbed him of his "rest." He longed to become a participant in the battle of the despoiled; he sought to leave the day-to-day routine of journalism as Phillips did, but Russell's motive was to enter the social conflict as his own man full-time. The power of the ethic he tried to teach Phillips, Russell later summed up himself: he hoped for his pupil to be "a democrat, socially and intellectually" and to make this philosophy "the fiber of his work and message."[36] Indeed, by 1907, Russell felt that their close companionship of *World* days had come to pay off very handsomely for popular novelist Phillips: "He has got hold of the ultimate Americanism in our life, he has seen the kind of men and women and young people that we have developed and the origin of their peculiarities, and he has perceived the controlling forces in the national existence. In this sense he is the most truly American of all our novelists."[37] The combined influence of Pulitzer and Russell on the creative esthetic of David Graham Phillips was significant. From Pulitzer emanated the excitement of social and political revelations to be made among the citadels of privilege; from Russell, the literary possibilities of writing about the fate and foibles of those caught in "the system." The ability to unify as a singular literary weapon the senses of the reporter and the sensibility of a reformer was to command much of Phillips' ambition. The fact that his perilous road of authorship led him along a path of mere external circumstances, and permitted him to see only the outermost pressures of individual suffering and social upheaval never occurred to—and so could not disturb—David Graham Phillips.

III The Great God Success

Perhaps frantic at the thought of being consigned to newspaper work for the remainder of his career as a writer ("for the newspaper which dies with the day of its date")[38] and fearful of having to be satisfied with "a mere Park Row reputation, but [not] the real thing,"[39] Phillips, shortly after the new century began, whipped himself spasmodically through a novel that dealt with the rough-and-tumble world of metropolitan journalism, *The Great God Success*. Because he was still affiliated with the *World*, Phillips brought out the novel pseudonymously as John Graham; but the backgrounds of the book came close to identifying its writer: "The author," stated H. E. Armstrong in *The Book-Buyer*, "is evidently a newspaper man who has done something more than serve an apprenticeship in the hard school which he describes. . . . The study repels, but a strong and a true hand has laid on the colors."[40] Charles Edward Russell delightedly noted the novel as "a clinic on the induration and fatty degeneration of the soul that invariably attend material achievement." "Every stage of the progress," he concluded, "was cleanly and evenly laid bare."[41]

The Great God Success is a novel both promising and absurd; its importance lies in the autobiographical materials on which the tale is based and in the primitive treatment of several themes that later came to be identified with Phillips. The story simply narrates an Alger-type tale that records a young rogue's progress "up the ladder." Howard climbs to the apex of the newspaper world; "sells out" to the Coal Trust; and, as reward for duplicity, terminates his career as an ambassador to France. A visitor to the embassy describes his portrait: "I see—a fallen man . . . hypocrisy, vanity, lack of principle, and, plainest of all, weakness. It's a common enough type among your successful men. The man himself is the fixed market price for a certain kind of success" (297-98).

Along the way to the diplomatic corps Howard encountered pretty much the same Park Row influences as his creator Phillips. Both had listened to the talk of newspaper professionals: "Journalism is not a career. It is either a school or a cemetery. A man may use it as a steppingstone. . . . But if he sticks to it, he finds himself an old man, dead and done for . . ."(11). Both had formulated a new dynamics of work and duty: "An intelligent plan, persisted in is hard to beat in this world of laggards and haphazard strugglers. . . . Work is the only permanently interesting thing in life . . . Work and sleep—the two periods of unconsciousness of self—are the two periods of happiness" (91, 93, 103).

Each also expressed "advanced" observations on free love and trial marriage in what Phillips called "a Bohemian quicksand":

"But are we not as good as married now?"
"Yes—that's it. And I want it to keep on. . . ."(71)

When, however, the novelist tried to wander away from the direct area of his personal and reportorial experience, the fiction became disastrous, especially in dialogue:

> "So much the more a scoundrel, he. . . . I think I would do well to look him up and give him a horse-whipping." (146-41)

> "You said you were engaged—pledged to another—that you could not draw back without dishonour." (190)

And the termination of Howard's affair with his mistress Alice is made in the succinct and abrupt manner that Frank Norris had developed as an underwritten supercharge:

> "Why, they've made you very gay this morning," he laughed, "with the red ribbons at your neck." There was no answer. He came still nearer. The red ribbons were long streamers of blood. She was dead. (81)

Phillips had exploited his world; the smell of printer's ink lingers through *The Great God Success,* and the rumor that the novel assassinated the character of an angry Joseph Pulitzer has little substance, because of the amazing similarities between Howard and Phillips himself. Pulitzer, in fact, commended Phillips for the novel in a cordial letter some time after the novelist and the *World* had parted company. The trend of the "romancer," as Pulitzer called his former prodigy, held a promise of long-term popularity that Phillips felt easily transcended in prestige the ephemeral nature of the dailies. Beveridge now began to urge; Carolyn began to persuade. And George Horace Lorimer, who had enjoyed John Graham's novel, beckoned. By 1902 Phillips was a free-lance writer. In the next nine years he would turn out more than twenty novels. He literally inundated the *Saturday Evening Post* with his productions.

IV *Beveridge and Lorimer*

In 1900 Albert J. Beveridge began his series of intermittent contributions to the *Post* which Lorimer had taken over a year before. Articles on imperialism and the Philippines, Cuba and Russia issued from his pen. Studies of Americanism and the duties of early twentieth-century patriots were also popular topics for the Senator to discuss: "You are an American, remember that. And be proud of it too. It is the noblest circumstance in your life. . . . Be American, therefore, to the uttermost limit of your consciousness and feeling. Thank God each day that your lot has fallen beneath the Stars and Stripes. It is a sacred flag. There is only one holier emblem known to man."[42] Beveridge also limned the virtues of the American home "where character is to be formed": ". . . yield yourself utterly to the mother. She has an instinctive perception of righteousness as affecting your character that no other intelligence under heaven has. . . ."[43]

The *Post* under Lorimer stressed "common honesty and common sense" in its content; essays published tended to be "bright, clever, [and] snappy"; the stories were "crackerjacks."[44] Not only did Phillips observe an admirable extension of the rugged Beveridge principles he had formerly come to admire as an undergraduate at DePauw, but he now saw in Lorimer—whose *Letters of a Self-Made Merchant to His Son* (1902) was described as preaching "that honesty is the best policy" and as illustrating this noble maxim "through the illumining medium of hog"[45]—a kind of Sunday-supplement Pulitzer whose literary shock-troops were interested in sketching the genteel happiness of a rather uncomplicated world through fiction that first appeared in the *Post* but that also eventually found its way between boards. Indeed, Lorimer went methodically about collecting his own particular entourage of productive writers: William Allen White, Owen Wister, Edwin Lefevre, F. Hopkinson Smith, Robert Chambers, and Frank Norris.[46]

Lorimer's appeal to the magazine-peddling "wide-awake boy" and to the iron-fisted American individualist dazzled Phillips with the racy, spellbinding quality that Benjamin Franklin had used in arresting the attention and capturing the minds of his middle-class Americans in quest of virtue and stability during changing times. Lorimer's Poor Richard, Jr., also knew the way to wealth and success:

Much doing is better than much learning.[47]

.   .   .   .

The man who takes things easy is the one who finds life hard.[48]

.   .   .   .

The world hates failures.[49]

. . . .

Pride costs. The bald-headed man pays as much for a haircut as anybody else.[50]

. . . .

A man who keeps himself in the pink of condition seldom has the blues.[51]

The *Post* also knew how to treat what it regarded as pretension and snobbery, characteristics unfortunately epitomized to a painful degree, the editors felt, by one of Edith Wharton's novels:

> *The House of Mirth* deals with a small set, within a small set, of New York society, who pride themselves on dressing like Parisians and living like Englishmen. Everything about them, down to their silly class pretensions, is made in England, France, or Germany. For nothing that is American have they the slightest use, except the dollar of their daddies. And in their reverence for that, they are European, not American.
>
> We repeat that we cannot see why the book is called a great American novel—we suppose it is called *The House of Mirth* because it is to laugh.[52]

In this intellectual milieu Phillips spent the remainder of his life. From the start of his free-lance career, Phillips exploded on America's literary scene with the same savage rate of production he always was to maintain. In May, 1902, *Her Serene Highness,* his second novel, was brought out by Harper's. In June, 1902, he published stories in *Success* and *Munsey's,* along with an article on Elihu Root in the *Post.* In September he brought out his third novel, *A Woman Ventures.* Fearful of a stagnancy or an inertia that would immobilize his intellect, Phillips never deviated from his self-imposed charge: work and sleep.

V Her Serene Highness

Her Serene Highness marked Phillips' only venture into historical fiction, and it was motivated by both his attraction for romance and his revulsion at the successful Graustarkian novels of the day. Picking up his pen with the purpose of satirizing out of existence the popular formula of George Barr Mc-Cutcheon and his followers of writing about mythical foreign kingdoms, Phillips unaccountably became enchanted with his own novel; and, forsaking satire, he himself contributed a rather flimsy, undistinguished literary specimen to the craze for Graustark-derived fiction.

Yet this perfumed tale of the love between Chicago art-collector Frederick Grafton and Princess Erica of Zweitenbourg contains two major themes that the novelist continued to exploit: the decadence of wealth and the woman in revolt. Grafton decimates the "death-in-life" of royalty, the degradation "of vanity and gilt," and the empty formalities of castle and throne. After much intrigue, flight, escape—even a duel—Erica happily elopes with her American lover. She has emphatically informed her wicked uncle that "life here [in the castle] is dull and repellent—a hell on earth, a mockery of a life, a torture-pen of yawning and meaningless routine" (168). Her new home is on Michigan Avenue.

Phillips secretly hoped that in perpetrating another Graustarkian romance on an already glutted market he might achieve the same type fame and royalties that had come to McCutcheon. Unfortunately for Phillips, his *Post* literary companion Owen Wister came out with *The Virginian* in 1902, a novel whose sale even surpassed the popularity of Myrtle Reed's *Lavender and Old Lace* and Charles Major's *Dorothy Vernon*. Phillips' historical effort was lost among such appealing competitors.

His tale in *Munsey's*, "That Person!" revolves about a similar theme: the calculated rejection of a fashionable existence among the *haut monde*, the "superior class." In the story, Gerald Blackwell of high society, proposes to Margaret Atherton (née Mary Cassidy), an actress. This bold step was taken against the advice of his socially-minded mother. But Margaret rejects Gerald: "I couldn't stand it. I couldn't stand the life; I couldn't stand the point of view. I'd be bored to death."[53] Thus, a "crowning indignity from 'that person'" was heaped upon the appalled and humiliated Mrs. Blackwell.

But in "Garlan and Company: A Wall Street Story," a tale in the area then being mined by another Lorimer protégé, Edwin Lefevre, one notes a sudden change in focus from the idle wealthy to the man of affairs, from the effete plutocrat to the captain of industry; in addition, this story dwells upon a theme that Phillips later explored as "the worth of a woman." In this story, Frederick M. Garlan, who lives in dissolute, reckless affluence, sees the firm "of which he is senior partner by inheritance" go bankrupt. This financial ruin, however, becomes the salvation of his marriage, for his wife maintained the same viewpoint as had Princess Erica and Mary Cassidy:

> "What has this monster down-town been but my worst enemy? Hasn't it taken you away from me? Hasn't it made you force upon me a mode of life that revolted all my better instincts, that would have changed me finally into a cold, heartless, wretched creature cut off from all the real joy there is in life? And I'm glad,—glad,—glad the monster is dead, is floating out of our lives like the great polluting, hideous thing that it is." [54]

VI A Woman Ventures

Even for a woman, the only redemption David Graham Phillips could perceive was work; leisure was corrosive; "luxury-hunting," as he described it, was an immoral passion. Thus the heroine of his next novel, *A Woman Ventures,* seeks her emancipation in journalism, as Phillips fleetingly returned to the newspaper world and traced the career, not of a "sob sister" but of a vigorous, talented reporter, Emily Bromfield, who, like the author, took postgraduate courses "at life's university" on city streets and who learned that "The price of freedom—to a woman just the same as a man—is work, hard work."[55]

This novel is, in reality, a love story with a Park Row background; and, just as he had done with the unconventional lovers, Alice and Howard, in *The Great God Success,* Phillips continued to chant a kind of experimental morality in "wicked" Bohemia. Emily informs Marlowe, a successful reporter in love with her: "'We will compromise with conventionality . . . we will marry, but we won't tell anybody. And I'll take an apartment with Joan Gresham and will go on with my work. . . . I don't want you as my husband. I want you to be my lover. And I want to be always, every time we meet, new and interesting to you'" (118).

Love and violence were the major materials exploited in *A Woman Ventures* by the enterprising novelist. When he was yet with the *Sun,* Phillips had distinguished himself in his coverage of a coal-mining strike with its despair and horror in the mountain country of Tennessee. Emily, similarly, undergoes her literal baptism of fire from behind a barricaded window in Furnaceville, Pennsylvania, as she covers an armed, bloody collision of capital and labor. Suddenly she is transformed from "a panic-stricken girl" to "a woman, confident of herself" (101). As several strikers are ruthlessly shot down, including one woman, Emily's colleague of the press, looking like "a maniac" with bulged, bloodshot eyes and "long yellow teeth ... grinding and snapping" erupted with the tension of the moment: " 'God damn them!' he shrieked. 'God damn the hell-hounds of the capitalists! Murderers! Murderers! killing honest workingmen and women!' " (100).

In this "man's world" that she successfully enters, Emily learns to respect the law of club and fang: " 'What does God care about us wretched little worms?' " she said to herself. " 'Everywhere the law of the survival of the fittest—the best law, after all, in spite of its cruelty' " (218). This Spencerian view begins to color her observations of New York slum and tenement life: "The stove was red-hot and two women in tattered, grease-bedaubed calico were sitting at it. They were young in years, but their abused and neglected bodies were already worn out. One held a child with mattered [sic] eyes and sores hideously revealed through its thin hair. The other was about to bring into the world a being to fight its way up with the rats and the swarming roaches" (240).

Yet Phillips keeps veering away from the theses that might make of *A Woman Ventures* fiction in the proletarian or Naturalistic tradition and weakly concentrates on Emily's love life, which ultimately becomes the most important aspect of his interest. Through her various romantic entanglements in the novel (antiseptic, although "daring"), Emily learns "to value freedom and self-respect" and to beware of "blind, reckless passion." The novel actually terminates with "the birds in the eaves [beginning] to chirp, to twitter, to sing" as Emily's true love returns to her. Thus *A Woman Ventures* descends to the very depths of extravagant sentimentalism, despite the author's carefully sketched backgrounds of authentic slum life and print-shop detail. Such dedication to truth was markedly in contrast to the synthetic turns of his plot.

"Thursday at Three," a tale Phillips placed in *McClure's* for December, closed his frenzied publication record of 1902. The current phenomenon of "title hunting," American women "mad" on the subject of foreign ancestry and lineage, was attractive to Phillips, who regarded Burke's *Peerage* as a catalogue of noble, wealthy ne'er-do-wells. He, as well as his colleagues Russell and Lorimer,[56] expressed harsh contempt for the refined, genteel American ladies whose major concerns were class and caste: "Mrs. Grant was a patron of arts and letters, as became a *grande dame* whom a freak of fate had condemned to one earthly pilgrimage as a common American woman."[57] Phillips' treatment of this social eccentricity was, perhaps, as superficial as the custom itself: title-seekers are shallow and un-American, he concluded. Yet he found this theme creeping boldly into many of his novels. Now, however, he had brought his first free-lance year to a close by treading those outskirts of human experience, by examining a relatively inconsequential aberration of the American "400" at the close of the nineteenth century.

With his own emancipation from Pulitzer and the *World*, Phillips quickly approached the problem of fiction with the certain step of the confident journalist whose knowledge of man he freely correlated with the insights and information gleaned from his frequent experiences in interviewing in police courts and drawing rooms. Phillips' emotional antennae had become attuned to the conflicts that lay behind many a tabloid story. In early tales and novels, he began his methodical job of probing the outer perimeter of man's consciousness; indeed, his later career in letters might have been forecast with a good deal of accuracy from a study of these early efforts and from one of his interests. Pulitzer had once urged Phillips to read *Crime and Punishment*;[58] instead, the renegade from journalism, interested in the Romances of the hour, turned to the *Saturday Evening Post*.

CHAPTER 3

Hearts and Masks

BETWEEN January, 1903, and November, 1906, David
Graham Phillips continued his feverish literary activity.
Scarcely a month passed without at least one of the popular or
esoteric American periodicals publishing one of his tales or
manifestoes. In *Everybody's Magazine* he described the business
tactics of "The Men Who Made the Steel Trusts";[1] in *Reader*
magazine he analyzed America's "Shifting Party Lines";[2] for the
Arena Phillips discussed "The New School of Socialism in
Europe";[3] for *Success* he evaluated "The Advance in the Cost of
Living";[4] and for the *Post,* in three issues scarcely more than one
month apart, he exposed "The Penalties of Poverty,"[5] "The
Penalties of Plutocracy,"[6] and "The Making of the City Slums."[7]
For *Appleton's, Collier's,* and *Cosmopolitan,* this compulsive
writer contributed articles on Tom Johnson,[8] The Great Balti-
more Fire,[9] and The Empire of Rothschild.[10]

When his pen was momentarily idle, Phillips meticulously
tracked down story material on the city streets in the company
of Val J. O'Farrell, owner of a Broadway detective agency
(with branches in Boston and Philadelphia), and with Alfred
Henry Lewis, another journalist and novelist then writing
popular fictional tracts of exposé like *The Boss* (1903), dedicated
to one George Horace Lorimer, and *The President* (1904).
Most frequently, however, Phillips was standing before his
"black pulpit"[11] turning out the copy; and, like the good
reporter that he was, most interesting to him were the contemporary dilemmas, domestic and business, that were prominent
in newspaper headlines, society columns, and police blotters.

This initial outburst of creative industry reached for Phillips
its emotional apex with the appearance of his controversial
articles arraigning America's "House of Dollars" in *The Treason*

of the Senate (*Cosmopolitan,* March-November, 1906). During this "pre-Treason" period, Phillips might be said to have composed two separate and distinct clusters of novels: one, a sequence of drawing-room dramas exposing hypocrisy of fashionable, as well as lower, society; the other, of much more consequence in the total canon of his work, a series of books depicting at close range the world of chance, politics, and business—an inquiry into the corrosive kinships of Power, the corrupt harmony and collusion existing in a plutocratic America between the various forces that manipulated contemporary society.

I Golden Fleece

The first novel David Graham Phillips serialized in the *Saturday Evening Post* was *Golden Fleece,* which began its run in January, 1903. Subtitled *The American Adventures of a Fortune-Hunting Earl,* the work contained all the ingredients that George Horace Lorimer could desire for success in his widely circulated magazine. Eleanor Hoyt, in her review, pinpointed the qualities most appealing not only to readers of the *Post* but also to those who purchased the hardbound edition released in April, 1903:

> "Golden Fleece" . . . is distinctly entertaining and indisputably clever. Incidentally, it is light—light as froth. Mr. Phillips would probably be the first to nod assent to this proposition. He had no intention of writing an epoch-making novel, but . . . a light, amusing satire upon certain American social conditions and he accomplished his purpose, putting into smiling arraignment [*sic*] an amount of keen observation and clever characterization that might well have equipped a much weightier and more important novel, had Mr. Phillips not chosen to toss the material gayly into a readable and ephemeral story. . . . The satire is good-humored but unsparing. . . .[12]

Especially attractive to Lorimer was the fact that Phillips reversed the social procedure then in vogue; instead of picturing American heiresses hopefully throwing themselves at the feet of the Earl of Frothingham, Phillips portrayed the scheming, innocuous Earl as casting about with growing desperation for a wealthy American wife. With an obvious contempt for the

Earl, as well as for the assortment of "parasites" and "plutocrats" the noble visitor encounters on his meanderings through the societies of New York, Boston, Washington, and Chicago, Phillips contrasts the dishonesty of the European and the Easterner with the plain, simple frontier virtues of the great plains: "You'd better go West if you wish to be sure of seeing the real thing" (58), the Earl is advised. He then is told how he can identify "this real American": "When you see a man or a woman who looks as if he or she would do something honest and valuable, who looks you straight in the eyes, and makes you feel proud that you're a human being and ashamed that you are not a broader, better, honester one—that's an American" (58).

There are some American girls, generally from New York, who "try to act a duchess out of one of Ouida's novels" (45); but, "fake culture" or not, the ladies are remarkably immune to the amorous assaults of poor, ineffectual Frothingham, who is finally rejected even by (*horribile dictu!*) Miss Jeanne Hooper of Chicago, heiress of "Hooper's High-Class Hams" and "Hooper's Excelsior Dressed Beef and Beef Extract." No doubt the national pride of each reader soared to emotional heights when Mr. Amzi Hooper asserted to the nobleman: "I won't bribe any man to marry my daughter. That ain't the American way" (285). Thus, after "seven months of stalking," after discovering that in this country—especially the West—"there were no idlers, no idling places," Frothingham leaves these "American upstarts" to their "beastly country" and returns to England where he marries his original sweetheart (grown wealthy through an inheritance during his absence) who is contentedly aware of the Earl's mercenary tendencies.

The *Arena* magazine noted that Phillips realized "the peril and promise of the present";[13] certainly the race for titles was a mere symptom of what he perceived as a somewhat larger social disorder: the concentration and entrenchment of privilege was antagonistic to his concept of democracy but not to his innate hatred of "aristocratic despotisms."[14] To a writer who embodied for B. O. Flower "the sturdy spirit of the old-time American democracy, the democracy of the Declaration of Independence and the fathers," the seduction of American ladies by the allurement and prestige of foreign titles was an ultimate anathema. Phillips, however, pictured the American girl, contrary

CARNEGIE LIBRARY
LIVINGSTONE COLLEGE
SALISBURY, N. C. 28144

DAVID GRAHAM PHILLIPS

to journalese cliché of the hour, as not completely susceptible
to foreign blandishments. His satire, while light, was essentially
humorless; for in each of this author's novels lay a serious
purpose—and the ability to be funny was not one of his talents.

II The Social Secretary

Lorimer's *Post* also serialized *The Social Secretary*, beginning
in February, 1905; and the novel appeared in boards "with
illustrations" and "decorations" in October. Similar in theme to
Golden Fleece, The Social Secretary offers a scrutiny of Washington society through the perceptive eyes of Miss Augusta
Talltowers, secretary to Mrs. "Ma" Burke, whose rustic husband
is a senator and whose plan is to learn the social amenities from
the knowledgeable Augusta. Phillips again scatters his general
anti-European sentiments throughout ("Eugenie is a dear, more
like an American than a foreigner" [85]), but he points up the
unbelievable complications of keeping a social calendar in
Washington. Augusta's bookkeeping includes entries in a Ledger,
a Day-Book, a Calling-Book, and a Ball-and-Big-Dinner Book;
and, while she undertakes her job with sophisticated vision, she
learns that launching "a fine stately ship . . . in this big-little sea
of Washington society" involves, primarily, not perceptive wisdom but promotion: organizing "the campaign thoroughly" (30,
167). She recognizes that the social clash is worse than armed
conflict, for in warfare there is at least respite between skir-
mishes: "This [however] is a continuous battle day and night,
week in and week out, with no let-up for Sundays" (96).

Again, however, Phillips blunts his theme and sacrifices a
purposeful direction for several love involvements. The passion
of Mr. Robert Gunton for an exotic *femme fatale* of early
twentieth-century Romantic fiction, Baroness Nadeshda Dara-
gane, "a wonder woman . . . in the flesh," evokes an inflamed
outburst of gallant, however unseemly, emotion: "Did you see
her night before last in that dress of silver spangles like the
wonderful skin of some amazing serpent? Did you see her eyes—
her hair—the way her arms looked—as if they could wind themselves round a man's neck and choke him to death while her
eyes were fooling him into thinking that such a death was
greater happiness than to live?" (109). And the Baroness herself

wails, "I must have him; I must be his slave" (115). Then, as one might guess, Augusta is pursued and finally captured by Cyrus Burke, eligible son of her employers. "Ma" Burke laughs and cries for joy.

Reviewers again stressed with justice the frothy image of the tale; and, while *Outlook* called *The Social Secretary* "distinctly clever and humorous,"[15] the New York *Times* carried this observation one step further: "Mr. Phillips's airy tale is a fascinating one, and, perhaps, if one looks closely, he may find beneath the daintily flavored meringue some food for thought."[16] Such food for thought, however, blatantly unseasoned, really needed little spice: the political social whirl was obviously a battleground strewn with victims, its inhabitants engaged in perpetual war with one another. Phillips later returned to explore this area from another vantage point in *The Fashionable Adventures of Joshua Craig* (1908), the novel directly responsible for his assassination.

In the story of Augusta Talltowers, however, Phillips showed his preoccupation with the prominent and fashionable; furthermore, his involvement with the materials of his fiction did not extend to the passionate concern for an individual as he endeavored to confront the small, tight inner core of life. Nor did he show an apprehension that personal identity could be achieved through a suffering awareness of the wounds such a confrontation can inflict. Phillips faced the problems of living as he would regard the front page of the New York *World*—with interest; and, since he constructed his work for appeal to the mass audience, solutions to many of his spiritually famished conflicts were slick, acceptable, and "happy." He was fixated by the literary necessity of weaving throughout most of his early novels a love story that dominated his total literary effort. Fortunately, he later learned to control his material with a surer hand; and, because of his sad notoriety stemming from the *Treason* articles, he was less concerned with mass appeal and approval.

III The Mother-Light

There was, too, in Phillips at this stage of his career in letters a highly ambitious element that led him to write and publish an anonymous novel, *The Mother-Light* (1905), set in a Trenton,

New Jersey, suburb; there were located "an extraordinary religious cult, something after the Theosophical order" and a high-priestess, "a Mme. Blavatsky" endowed with "psychic powers, and immortal youth and beauty."[17] From Paris, Phillips wrote of this project in a letter to Lorimer: "I've a notion that you could give me a very valuable criticism of the Light. . . . my sister is inclined to agree with you that I ought to let it go anonymously and as it stands—But I have a feeling that somehow there is more of a story in it than I've brought out and that I ought to build around my plot a study of the religious conditions in America—and I think I'll try, though I may go back finally to what I already have."[18]

His sights set high, Phillips a short time later informed Lorimer from Biarritz that he had rewritten *The Mother-Light* "almost entirely" ("I won't say it's better, but I will say it's different. . . ."),[19] but his plan to treat religious conditions in America was clearly abortive. Lorimer, certainly, would have had little sympathy with such a novel, for his simple American "gospel of wealth" as advertised in the *Post* through the wisdom of Poor Richard, Jr., would lean away from any probe into so hallowed and explosive an area as the cathedral of worship; for he had written: "Of buildings that represent the good in life, first comes the church, second the schoolhouse, and third the savings-bank. And all three prosper in the United States."[20] Thus any novel failing to concentrate on the high correlation of respectable church membership among the captains of industry in America would have been unpalatable to Lorimer and to his army of subscribers; but, in any event, Phillips' original design went amiss.

Rather than an exploration of religious sentiment or conditions in America, *The Mother-Light* was merely nebula of a quasi-religious nature; that is, the work became a love story enacted against a background of contemporary religious aberration. Basis for the plot might be uncovered in studies of Mary Baker Eddy, along with the legends and folklore surrounding her career in Christian Science; for Mrs. Eddy, eighty-four years old when Phillips apparently used her as his fictional model, had built, organized, and publicized "the Mother Church" until it became "the largest and most powerful organization ever founded by any woman in America." A virtual deity herself, she symbolized for her devotees "their temporal as well as their spiritual ruler."[21]

In the Phillips novel suggested by the controversial Mrs. Eddy is Ann Banks, an elderly priestess, who had discovered a new religion of Happiness and had set down the principles in her book, THE WAY OF THE LIGHT: "Time, Space, Matter, Death, Disease, Sin—all these are the delusions of the Darkness. That which takes away their power over the immortal Mind puts in their place a *present* eternity of Life and Health. The Light gives Health of Body no less than Health of Soul. It banishes all forms of sin. It purifies the soul—the Mind—and thus enables the Mind to electrify the body forever as in childhood" (30).

This female Messiah, the Mother-Light, however, is in poor health; and Maida Claflin Hickman, a widow from Ida Grove, Iowa, who has heard the call of "Destiny," is groomed to take Ann's place, for the interior circle of zealots in this sect demands that The Mother be perpetuated. Maida is almost rescued from this fanaticism by Dr. Gayland Thorndyke, who has fallen in love with her ("Come away with me to safety and sunshine" [283]). But Maida now has a holy mission; and, uttering the incantations of her faith, she rejects her lover: "May The Light shine in you! May your blasphemy be forgiven!" (283). The probing of the religious demon in the American consciousness resolves itself in an adventurous love story with a pseudo-theological background as Phillips is interested mainly in revealing Maida's vanity, her conflict with the Light and her passion. The feeling of power that comes to her when the masses of devout are groveling at her feet will be ample compensation for her lost suitor.

Reasons for the author's desired anonymity, however, relate in some way to Lorimer's objections to the novel; for the sage of the *Post* noted sentiments in the book that could alienate Phillips' considerable magazine following. In several scenes in *The Mother-Light,* Phillips personally spoke out in the words of Dr. Thorndyke, a dedicated man of science, and expressed ideas that might jeopardize a luminous public image: "The dreamer, pursuing his dream to prove that it is no dream, finds out at last the frightful truth. He goes to the source of the Soul, makes the long and weary search back through the infinity of aimless sequences into which man used to read intelligent causation. He comes at last, not to the laboratory of an Infinite Intelligence, but to the idle commotions of a soulless, mindless, inanimate ocean" (216). Life is "A nightmare of hate and fear and cruelty and murder, interrupted here and there with the splendid, pitiful dreams of a life of peace beyond." Imagination is a "tragic accident" that is "turned by blind force" into "infinite combinations of trivialities" (217). "Ignorance," thundered Dr. Thorndyke, "can wonder and worship, but—what is there for Intellect but despair?"

Emanating from an author whose mind critics equated with the intellect of a revered President, whose words spoke "earnestly and with an iteration almost Rooseveltian,"[22] these views could joggle the minds of conventional readers and, possibly, disillusion many enthusiasts of Phillips' early froth. Thus *The Mother-Light* was orphaned at birth, and, because it again shies away from the larger issues implicit in any analysis of contemporary religious thought, the novel belongs topically to its author's explorations of the fringe interest popular readers might have in some American social anomalies pervading the scene. His major source still remained the daily newspaper; this reservoir of notable experiences would never fail David Graham Phillips.

IV The Fortune Hunter

Vanity, snobbery, cant, and deceit, however, were not the private property of the Madison Avenue set or of the suburbanite religious pilgrim; and in *The Fortune Hunter* (1906), Phillips turned his attention to the sidewalks of New York to whip up lathers of froth among the lower depths. It was a literary vogue of the day for a given journalist to appropriate a portion of Manhattan Island as his own private fictional property and to mine this area of its types, traditions, and dialect: "For Greenwich Village, Washington Square and the lower west side there are Bunner, Brander Matthews, Janvier; for the Ghetto, Cahan; for Murray Hill, Richard Harding Davis; for curious, out-of-the-way nooks on the island's eastern brink, Henry Harland. . . ."[23]

Phillips' former colleague of the *Sun*, Rudolph Edgar Block ("Bruno Lessing"), was contributing a series of local-color tales of lower New York life to many of the same periodicals advertising the work of Phillips, who now reclaimed his identity and turned to the recent immigrant in what *Critic* called a "Rather clever ... sketch of ... [a] social nuisance."[24] Carl Feuerstein, the fortune hunter, is not a royal foreigner; he is a penniless actor, albeit a "romantic figure" of the German Theater stock company of the lower East Side. Like his ineffectual, scheming counterpart, the Earl of Frothingham, he is, however, shamelessly in quest of a rich wife and intrigues to marry Hilda Brauner, whose father operates a thriving delicatessen store on Avenue A. Miss Brauner, "healthy and vigorous and useful as well as beautiful," and her "true lover" Otto Heilig, who is just starting in the delicatessen business, are victimized by the rogue Feuerstein. Hilda, for a time, believes in the actor's honesty and declared love until he is ultimately unmasked as a bigamist and a swindler who had eloped with Lena Ganser, daughter of a wealthy uptown brewer at the very time he was courting gullible Hilda. The termination of Mr. Feuerstein's colorful off-stage career is brought to a startling conclusion in Meinert's Beer Garden on Sixth Street: "He took the knife, held it at arm's length, blade down. He turned his head to the left and closed his eyes. Then with a sudden tremendous drive he sent the long narrow blade deep into his neck. The blood spurted out, his breath escaped from between his lips with long, shuddering, subsiding hisses. His body stiffened, collapsed, rolled to the floor. Mr. Feuerstein was dead—with empty pockets and the drinks unpaid for" (179-180). Otto and Hilda will now marry; and, dedicated to "work and love and home," they will soon be free from "the shadow of Mr. Feuerstein—of vanity and false emotion, of pose and pretense" (214).

Phillips notes in *The Fortune Hunter* that sham and hypocrisy exist as much in the underprivileged area around Tompkins Square as in "a drawing-room full of culture-hunters farther uptown" (56). He also excoriates lawyers as professional malingerers: "They defended thieves and murderers; they prosecuted or defended scandalous divorce cases; they packed juries and suborned perjury and they tutored false witnesses.... In private life they were ... home-loving, law-abiding citizens" (93). But, despite the occasional stab at affectation, the tale of love among "imported sausage and fish ... chicken livers and spiced meats" (13) is more waste than substance. The good journalist has painted a credible, amusing background; but the ever-dominating love tale limited the scope and the range of the novel. *The Fortune Hunter*,[25] epitomizes the "breezy" aspect of Phillips' fiction. Exhibiting a journalese vitality, he assaulted some common vices and hypocrisies with the uncompromising vigor of a syndicated columnist. Yet, during this time, he was bringing out a more significant type of fiction, one that merged very closely with the conscience of humanity rather than its curiosity. In addition to exposing some popular manifestations of American "*Kultur*," he was also probing at its foundations.

V   The Reign of Gilt

Aside from the "Rooseveltian" muscularity that some critics felt he was expressing in his fiction, Phillips organized for publication in 1905 a collection of essays that brought completely into focus the philosophy motivating his life and work until the appearance of his *Treason* articles. *The Reign of Gilt* was divided into two sections, Plutocracy and Democracy; and, amid eye-catching chapter titles ("Caste-Compellers," "Pauper-Making," "Democracy's Dynamo") it offered a *tour de force* that culminated in a magniloquent apotheosis to Intelligence, Democracy, and the Common Man. The *Arena*, always sympathetic (generally rhapsodic) to Phillips, urged buying the book as a patriotic duty: "Therefore, we say that he who loves the republic should buy, read and circulate 'The Reign of Gilt.' The more such books are circulated, the more certainly and swiftly will come the democratic reaction for which we are all striving."[26] Phillips' wholesale attack on Privilege, his brutal investigation of Mr. and Mrs. Multi-Millionaire, and his lurid description of New York decadence gave the impression that he was a crusader for Equality and Truth.

The Reign of Gilt is useful as a handbook of Phillips' major patterns of thought, as well as of the literary materials he exploited in fiction. The mania for gilt, stressed Phillips, has led incipient and accomplished fiscal plunderers to New York, "the capital of our plutocracy": "Into it are pouring wealth and luxury, pictures, statuary and works of art of all kinds and periods; jewels and collections of rarities. In it are rising miles and miles of palaces, wonderful parks and driveways. It has begun to be a City Splendid" (70). The luxury-hunting, luxury-teaching economy threatens to destroy America, so frantic is the competitive pursuit of gilt: "In the neighborhood of these pluto-crats and their parasites and imitators, struggling thus desperately in gaudiness, it is all but impossible not at times to fear that prosperity, concentrated prosperity, has killed Democracy, has killed the republic. Foreigners look at New York amid the galaxy of rich cities eagerly imitating it, and shrug their shoulders and sneer" (31).

The prevalent standard of conspicuous consumption, as Thor-stein Veblen had coined the phrase a few years earlier, afflicted an effete leisure class, a "plutocracy" sighing "in vain for trans-formation into an aristocracy" (39). To achieve "power without effort" (103), to create vast dependencies ("pauper-making"), and to purchase very casually "inequality and ... privilege" (16) are marks of the current "money-maniacs." With painful thoroughness Phillips presented an account book (not doc-umented) of a typical family living in "a palace of white marble, in Fifth Avenue, near Fifty-ninth Street" across from Central Park: "Up to the present time it has cost them two and a half millions, and that does not include the one hundred and seventy-five thousand dollar set of tapestries for the dining-room. . . . The site cost half a million; the house three quarters of a million . . ." (32).

This plutocracy, asserted Phillips, "descended ... swift as a cyclone, insidious as a plague," and "cure-alls so confidently proposed by our political and sociological quacks" (137) seem both futile and disastrous. Patience and Democracy will in the future, the author suggests, ease this horrible blight upon the land and lead to the abolition of caste on this side of the Atlantic. Thus concluded Part I of *The Reign of Gilt* in which Phillips had arraigned the monster of the moment; but, unlike the reformer, he was more intent on the drama of his indictment than on inciting the "class struggle." The vast suffering humanity that Jacob Riis, Jane Addams, Robert Hunter, and Ray Stannard Baker were bleeding with was never personalized by Phillips. A coldness, a clinical, professional, business-like prose devoid of emotion purveyed his simple thesis; the other side of the tracks was not adequately studied.

In Part II, which begins with "We, the People," Phillips advances the thesis that, for a valid, uncolored view of real, grass-roots America, "we must leave the neighborhood of the palaces of the plutocracy" and "we must also leave the neighboring slums, where the American is so sadly caricatured." The disinterested investigator must study "the smaller cities and the towns and villages and the farms, where in ten thousand homes a sane and sober life is led by a sane and sober people" (142). In this so-called Valley of Democracy, there is no vestige of "the European idea of deference" (146), no manifestation of "Snobism" (148). Class is rejected in favor of the "energetic and progressive" mass (147). Phillips momentarily sounds like a prophet of America's future eminence—like a Reform Darwinian who, in the heat of passion, strikes for changing the forces moulding our iniquitous *status quo*. But Phillips would stop short of assuming a political stance too far removed from conservative dead-center; and, by way of compensation for his "radical" onslaughts against the masters of capital, he heaped strong critical abuse on Thorstein Veblen, "the compeller of equality."

Phillips' execration of Veblen's style and ideas in *The Theory of Business Enterprise* (1904) is not difficult to explain, for he felt that this "Professor" was an intellectual snob with "a passionate ... predilection for polysyllables" (162). That Veblen was pushing Reform Darwinian economics into a fierce critique of the modern businessman and the machine process, Phillips perceived and resented. That the profit motive was analyzed by Veblen as having more importance to the businessman than the philanthropic gesture of making goods available, Phillips either blindly rejected or foolishly did not understand. He had found the self-made captains of industry merely amusing and autocratic; Veblen found them predatory, vicious, and unsympathetic. Phillips up to this time had dealt with the plutocrats in a vacuum that shielded his thought from "the despairing cry of children," "the daughters of the poor," and "the woman who works." Veblen synthesized the economic criticism to include all of the social contract on all levels. Veblen's definition of Conservative doubtless seemed as a personal insult to Phillips and his associates on the *Post:*

The business classes are conservative, on the whole, but such a conservative bent is, of course, not peculiar to them. These occupations are not the only ones whose reasoning prevailingly moves on a conventional plane. Indeed, the intellectual activity of other classes, such as soldiers, politicians, the clergy, and men of fashion, moves on a plane of still older conventions; so that if the training given by business employments is to be characterized as conservative, that given by these other, more archaic employments should be called reactionary. Extreme conventionalization means extreme conservatism. Conservatism means the maintenance of conventions already in force.[27]

Veblen pilloried the "machine process" and its encouragement of "conspicuous waste": "The ubiquitous presence of the machine, with its spiritual concomitant—workday ideals and skepticism of what is only conventionally valid—is the unequivocal mark of the Western culture of today. . . . The working population is required to be standardized, movable, and interchangeable in much the same impersonal manner as the raw or half-wrought materials of industry."[28]

In *The Reign of Gilt* Phillips presented many random quotes from *The Theory of Business Enterprise* to line up better his sights for counterattack on "Professor Veblen . . . [who] is putting into scientific formula the sneer of every snob who professes contempt of business and, indeed, of all other forms of modern democratic activity" (163). He chides Veblen for relying in his research "upon the poets and poetical historians" (167); he is irritated at Veblen's respect for books as contrasted with his own "keyhole" experience. This resentment is interesting in that Phillips later did little serious researching for his own *Treason* articles, but was supplied with facts by a "team." In *The Reign of Gilt*, however, he speaks without authority, even vaguely and erroneously, about "the fast disappearing sweatshops" on New York's Lower East Side; and he grimly laments: "The poets have it otherwise; and so do those historians who like to paint alluring pictures for their readers—and hate to grub for facts. But there is the grisly truth" (168).

These wild contentions are positively incredible in the light of some very capable "fact grubbers" writing alongside David Graham Phillips and publishing in widely circulated journals in the same era. George Kibbe Turner's "The Daughters of the

Poor" (*McClure's,* 1909) noted with mordant agitation that "... from the population of 350,000 Jews east of the Bowery tens of thousands of young girls go out into the shops. There is no more striking sight in the city than the mass of women that flood east through the narrow streets.... The exploitation of young women as money-earning machines has reached a development on the East Side of New York probably not equalled anywhere else in the world!"[29] Edwin Markham's portrait of "Spinners in the Dark" (*Cosmopolitan,* July, 1907) also leads one to question the basis for Phillips' outburst in behalf of the emancipated worker:

> Inside the mill there is the constant strain of young muscle matched against untiring machinery. The children at the frames must stand all night, always alert, always watching for broken threads, nimble to let no loose end be caught in with other threads.... The floors of woolen-mills are always slippery with wool grease. [A] child slipped, and thrusting out her arm she was caught in the cogs of an unguarded machine.... But like the children blinded by splintering glass or the children struck by flying shuttles ... this girl goes to fill up that black page of statistics....[30]

What David Graham Phillips saw was the triumph of the gospel of wealth in the present, the scientific veracity of Conservative Darwinism. In fact, Phillips was seduced by the apothegm he frequently was to satirize: "Godliness is in league with riches." He aligned his feelings with the sentiments expressed by the Right Reverend William Lawrence in 1901: "Put two men in adjoining fields, one man strong and normal, the other weak and listless. One picks up his spade, turns over the earth and works till sunset. The other turns over a few clods, gets a drink from the spring, takes a nap, and loafs back to his work. In a few years one will be rich for his needs, and the other a pauper dependent on the first, growling at his prosperity."[31]

Phillips often expressed variations on his fundamental belief that "Hard work is the prime condition of achievement"; he tended to idolize the "self-made" intellectual sinews that chanted "work; work hard! Be a somebody..." (232). Thus in *The*

Reign of Gilt he set down a doctrine of conscientious conservatism unembarrassed by the facts of the present:

> In place of a world where all but a handful toiled early and
> late—from dawn until far into the night—toiled that others might
> reap all and they only blows and the meagre bread of bitterness,
> we now have a world where millions upon millions are comfort-
> able. And as for the masses and toilers still in the shackles of
> the old regime, are they not better off than they were under
> that regime where wages were alms, and alms of the scantiest?
> (168-69)

The machine Phillips regards as salvation; the business man "is
in control" and "the worker's instincts" must be developed—
must be, especially, insulated against "unsubstantial ... false
ideals, fraudulent culture and barren fiddle-faddle of closet
theorizings" (181). "This gospel," he concludes, "will not be
attractive to *poseurs* and to the lazy and the incompetent. But
it is gospel, the gospel of Democracy, America's gospel" (182).

The remainder of *The Reign of Gilt* contains a varied series
of appraisals of Democracy with much enthusiastic rhetoric but
little theoretical substance. "Democracy's Dynamo" (education
in "the temple of reason"); "Not Generosity, But Justice" (phi-
lanthropists should not give alms; rather, dispense "justice");
"The Real American Woman" (no plaything, no "tenement 'sill-
warmer' or palace parasite," but a hard worker before and after
marriage)—all these treat different phases of Phillips' thesis:
Democracy triumphant. His Democracy, however, little resem-
bled the political philosophy of fellow Middle-Westerner John
P. Altgeld, despite Phillips' final panegyric to Abraham Lincoln
and to the Common Man ("You with your stout heart and your
willing and capable hands. You with your active, intelligent
brain" [293]). The future dawns before author Phillips with an
inspiring glitter that beckons to prosperity and "bright promise."

It is apparent that David Graham Phillips, though a remarkably well-informed journalist, was rather backward as a political
philosopher, unsystematic and naïve. Unable to organize his
socio-political theories into a coherent, consequential pattern,
his views are, to say the least, anachronistic and, at times, downright contradictory. Writing in the *Arena* (March, 1905) on

Socialism, he asserted: "To deny it is to refuse to read the plain pointing of the vanes in the wind of human destiny. Universal suffrage; the poor and the toiling overwhelmingly in the majority ... the electorate slowly awakening to its power through the ballot; capitalism setting the example of concentration and the use of the State for private enrichment...."[32] It seems evident that Phillips was interested in the arena of politics, economics, and the democratic processes as potential literary subjects, as a running story file organically formed with built-in aggressions and conflicts. He saw only the drama; he envisioned only his prose—propelling, quick, and moving. He liked the thought of being a verbal virtuoso, a literary demagogue of the printed page; and he would adapt any political posture of the moment to intensify a climactic, emotional impetus for the thesis he happened to be discussing. His pen was for hire; his sentiments altered with the characters in his fiction, carrying Phillips into a shadowy maze of inconsistency that defies orderly analysis.

In terms of his seriously considered fiction, this manner of literary operation had salient consequences. Phillips employed an equally unsystematic process in planning his novels: "It was characteristic of Mr. Phillips's methods not only to start from some person or incident having no real bearing on his story, but even after he had his story well plotted and his characters outlined, to be by no means sure what they were likely to do when the crisis came, or how the book was going to end."[33] On more than one occasion, apparently, "the characters took the matter quite out of his hands."[34] One could never predict how Phillips would sketch a robber-baron or politician. He may invest his characters with a scientifically controlled behavior pattern that raises to heights the theses of social Darwinists and other purveyors of the business ethic generated by the Herbert Spencer–Andrew Carnegie intellectual combine. At another moment he will reject completely this cosmic view and go on to praise honesty, decency, and morality in terms reflecting the position of a muckrake editorial from *McClure's*. The Common Man and the giant of finance occasionally became the "lion" and the "lion tamer."[35] Phillips, as his characters snapped the whip, employed metaphoric allusions in casual theology ("God is commanding him to destroy me"),[36] pseudo-philosophy ("the relentless, sure-aiming hunter, Fate")[37] and prodigal melodrama ("On the floor [dead] in the heaps and coils of ticker-tape lay Dumont").[38]

As a Romancer, Phillips was interested first and foremost in telling a readable and timely story. A unified scheme of thought and an integrated philosophical view were to him unnecessary luxuries, futile encumbrances. Moreover, Phillips might frequently endeavor to antagonize a reader, but he hoped never to alienate one. Such literary acrobatics even he found difficult to perform in the fictional amphitheater he soon entered.

CHAPTER 4

Fools and Their Money

I The Master Rogue

I WILL TELL my story myself," begins *Roger Drake, Captain of Industry* (1902), a novel by Henry Kitchell Webster, one minor scribbler who was making literary capital of the current interest in high finance, railroad regulation, and bucket-shop manipulation of the stock market.[1] And James Galloway, protagonist of *The Master Rogue* (1903), begins his first-person narrative in a similarly revealing manner but the statement is more immersed in the basic theme of the novel: "I cannot remember the time when I was not absolutely certain that I would be a millionaire."

Galloway's quick rise to riches, his passion for wealth, and his unscrupulous means for attaining it are related by the hero himself with an aplomb and a candor reminiscent of the "plain talks" by George Washington Plunkitt, scion of Tammany Hall, whose lectures on "Honest Graft and Dishonest Graft" appeared collected in a book in 1905: "He Seen His Opportunities, and He Took 'Em."[2] Galloway "seen" his opportunities too, and was forever buoyed by his intuitive knowledge that "Nature intended [him] for larger things" (10). By "sheer force of intellect" he succeeds in raising himself "above the mass of ... fellow men" (25), and he revels "dazzlingly above the dull mass of work-a-day people with their routines of petty concerns."

Galloway respects his success as much as he appreciates his own philanthropy: "I am a liberal man. My large gifts to education and charity ... prove it beyond a doubt" (57). As he almost effortlessly travels the pathway of plunder, his formerly "inexperienced conscience" (163) ceases to trouble him with its "hair-splittings." Denounced in the reformist press ("wretched rag") as "a swindler, and robber—worse, as an assassin," Galloway merely contemplates changing his public relations set-up. He annihilates business opposition, buys senators, demeans and humiliates his associates; his universe is the world of the social Darwinist: "Our wills had met in final combat. I saw that I must crush him—the one human being who dared to oppose me and defy me. . . ." Galloway dies, "one of the noblest men that ever lived," and his daughter bequeathes to posterity the James Galloway Memorial Museum of Art, although, ironically, during his lifetime the baron had dismissed cultural enlightenment as an affront to his single mind: "I don't care for pictures or that sort of thing. . . . I know that most of this talk of 'art' and the like is so much rubbish and affectation . . ." (66-67). Thus Phillips allows Galloway to confess with damning self-incrimination his own essential corruption and vanity and to present a world view that is totally predatory and rapacious. *The Master Rogue,* furthermore, can stand as Phillips' prologue to a triad of novels that purport to examine and expose plutocracy, political marauding, and social parasitism; for James Galloway is a full-blown financial brigand whose backgrounds and manipulations are chronicled from the very start of his unholy career in theft. His philosophy is opposed only by the author's irony, not by any antagonist in the novel. Phillips presented a roughed-out design of the universe in which Galloway operated and crudely sketched a variety of situations and circumstances (buying a husband for his daughter, subverting legislators, indulging parasites) that he later elaborated and studied in the novels flowing freely from his pen.

II The Cost

Writing in the San Francisco *Examiner,* Bailey Millard, soon to be chief instigator of *The Treason of the Senate,* reviewed *The Cost* (1904), which had been serialized in the *Post* and which was being advertised as "A Romance of the Dollar Mark."[3] The editor responded with a moving testimonial to a book that explored the socio-political climate from St. X, Indiana, to Wall Street: "It is a story full of virile impulse. It treats of men of hardy endeavor, battling for leadership in the world of commerce and politics. If you want a novel that is intensely modern and intensely full of speed and spirit, you have it in *The Cost*."[4] Wallace Rice of the Chicago *Examiner* regarded it as a "masterly novel, interesting to the point of fascination, analytic to the point of keenness. . . ."[5] as Phillips plunged recklessly into the wild vortex of corporate politics and romance.

But if *The Master Rogue* had presented a faithful, however dull, tintype of the contemporary scoundrel, *The Cost* gave a roseate picture of political saint Hampden Scarborough, whose prototype was Senator Albert J. Beveridge. On the final pages Scarborough and Pauline Gardner Dumont, who through a varied assortment of superficial and contrived circumstances, had managed to elude each other, are brought happily together: "In the following June came Scarborough. She was in the garden, was waiting for him, was tying up a tall rose. . . ." The antagonist in the tale is one John Dumont, who spirits young Pauline off to an early marriage, becomes a Wall Street titan, and sets up a corrupt chain of command between himself, his "puppet peoples and puppet politicians" (241). Wealth leads Dumont to a life of flagrant self-indulgence and physical gratification. Pauline, who feels both violated and disillusioned, leaves him: "She sat down before him in a low chair . . . her eyes never leaving his swollen, dark red, brutish face—a cigar stump, much chewed, lay upon his cheek near his open mouth. He was as absurd and as repulsive as a gorged pig asleep in a wallow" (129).

Being named as a corespondent in a sensational New York divorce case exploited to the fullest by a local scandal sheet of wide circulation begins the public dissolution of Dumont's image as a reputable financier. His "disgrace" encourages enemies to "raid for control" his holdings. Millionaire Dumont's mind deteriorates; he botches a half-hearted suicide attempt, but subsequently rallies from his hospital bed to wrest control of the company once more. He becomes "a wicked wolf, impatient to resume the life of the beast of prey" (364): "Than John Dumont, president of the Woolens Monopoly, there was no firmer believer in the gospel of divine right—the divine right of this new race of kings, the puissant lords of trade" (373). The "imperial destiny" of Dumont, however, betrays him—as does "his ambition for wealth and power"; strangled to death by coils of stock-market ticker-tape, in his "wine-colored wadded silk dressing-gown and white silk pajamas," the "fallen king" dies, a bizarre symbol of conspicuous futility: "In his struggles the tape had wound round and round his legs, his arms, his neck. It lay in a curling, coiling mat, like a serpent's head, upon his throat, where his hands clutched . . ." (399).

Dumont's world was that of James Galloway, the universe of colliding Forces, a crawling jungle; and Dumont himself had the demeanor of "a wild beast": "For the code enacted by ordinary human beings to guide their foolish little selves he had no more respect than a lion would have for a moral code enacted by and for sheep. The sheep might assert that their code was for lions also; but why should that move the lions to anything but amusement?" (372).

Less interesting than the decline and fall of John Dumont is the parallel story of "demi-god" Hampden Scarborough, whose pontifical expressions of Americanism reach inspirational heights. His moral power grows and expands as Dumont's arc of activity becomes more and more restricted until it is compressed, cold and lifeless, in the serpentine ticker-tape. Scarborough and Pauline had been in love when both were undergraduates at Battle Creek University, and her sudden marriage to Dumont had for a time left Scarborough an emotional wreck. Then, recovering his essentially stable equilibrium, he had plunged diligently into his work as book agent and law clerk; he advised: "Put yourself, your *best* self, into it" (144). Unlike Dumont, Scarborough scorns wealth: "I've no desire to be rich. It's too easy, if one will consent to give money-making his exclusive attention" (147).

Scarborough, with his silver tongue, became the reform candidate for governor. Christ-like, he explained to Pauline some of the political temptations dangled before him by "two corrupt rings": "Then they came to me . . . and took me up into a high mountain and showed me all the kingdoms of the earth as it were. I could be governor, senator, they said, could probably have the nomination for president even, not if I would fall down and worship them, but if I would let them alone" (218). In truth, Hampden Scarborough is a deity, powerful and tender, a Quixotic sentimentalist, one who speaks with a moving reverence about "the stars and the moon" (221).

On the other hand, a Dumont crony points out the universe

as recognized by the plutocracy: a cosmos reducing man and his dignity to the protoplasmic motes of biological determinism. No regard for the beauties of the firmament has he: "Those stars irritate me.... They make me appreciate that this world's a tiny grain of sand adrift in infinity, and that I'm—there's nothing little enough to express the human atom where the earth's only a grain. And then they go on to taunt me with how short-lived I am and how it'll soon be all over for me—forever. A futile, little insect, buzzing about, waiting to be crushed under the heel of the Great Executioner" (182).

In *The Cost,* too, Phillips extended his metaphor of war to include not only the social scheme of fashionable America but also the perilous world of finance: "Instead of shot and shell and regiments of 'cannon food,' there are battalions of capital, the paper certificates of the stored-up toil or trickery of men; instead of mangled bodies and dead, there are minds in the torment of financial peril or numb with the despair of financial ruin. But the stakes are the same old stakes—power and glory and wealth for a few ..." (387). The "cost" is simply the price for a man's freedom; the invoice for success; the tribute a leader of civilization must pay.

Phillips also juxtaposed not only two symbolic prototypes of the times but also counterpointed two divergent "Scriptures": the Gospel of Christ and the Gospel of Greed. American philosopher Charles S. Peirce defined the issue in this way: "The gospel of Christ says that progress comes from every individual merging his individuality in sympathy with his neighbors. On the other side, the conviction ... that progress takes place by virtue of every individual's striving for himself ... and trampling his neighbor under foot whenever he gets a chance to do so."[6] Dumont, a gratuitous, pathological monster peculiar to his times, is clearly a votary of what Peirce terms "the Gospel of Greed." Scarborough, in addition to following "in His steps," is a "sentimentalist": one who pays, as Peirce puts it, "great respect ... to the natural judgments of the sensible heart."[7] David Graham Phillips was deeply involved with both Dumont and Scarborough; he made his choice. Triumphing over man's plutocratic vision in a world where corruption of principle cleared a path toward mastery of one's fellows was the courageous Scarborough, whose major attractions to Phillips were his zeal for hard work, his romantic tenderness of soul, and his peerless honesty.

III The Plum Tree

The Plum Tree (1905), serialized in *Success Magazine*, might well bear the subtitle, "The Return of Hampden Scarborough," who here continues his political pilgrimage in the path of Christ by again eschewing temptations and by driving the money-lenders from the temple: "I purpose to continue to do what I can to break up the mob that is being led on by demagogues disguised as captains of industry and advance agents of prosperity—led on to pillage the resources of the country, its riches and its character" (276). For most of Scarborough's political contemporaries in the novel, however, "compromises between theoretical and practical right . . . are part of the daily routine of active life" (26): "The plum tree! Is there any kind of fruit which gladdens the eyes of ambitious man, that does not glisten upon some one of its many boughs, heavy-laden with corporate and public honors and wealth?" (145). Yet, by maintaining his deadly righteousness, the former law clerk of Saint X is nominated by "the convention" to be its presidential candidate. He is supported by "men who hated and feared him, but who dared not flout the people and fling away victory" (380). As President Hampden Scarborough, he speaks with the cant of mid-nineteenth-century perfectionism: "Man isn't a falling angel, but a rising animal. So, every impulse toward the decent, every gleam of light, is a tremendous gain. The wonder . . . isn't that we are so imperfect, but that in such a few thousand years we've got so far—so far up" (384).

Phillips guided readers of *The Plum Tree* through devious ward politics to the interior of the White House; yet the career of Scarborough is not his central focus in the novel. In *The Cost* he had counterpointed Governor Scarborough with John Dumont, financier and plutocrat; now he studied a contrast in political morality between Hampden Scarborough, a faultless, wise statesman, and one Harvey Sayler, a back-room manipulator and dictatorial kingmaker.

Sayler and Scarborough both had begun their legal careers in the same straitened circumstances, but Harvey had rebelled against his father's "old fashioned notions of honor and honesty" which brought Sayler, Sr., nothing but virtuous defeat in politics. Harvey rebelled too against a genteel poverty (which has the "power to make one afraid" [28]), and he began to court the profitable favors of Boss Bill Dominick, local ruler of the party usually in power. Ambitious Sayler soon outgrows "brute," "beast" Dominick (109) and becomes a liaison-man between the plutocrats, legislators, and bosses of the state. He makes a fortuitous marriage, forsaking Elizabeth Crosby, his childhood sweetheart who loves him; and he embarks on a cold-blooded career of political nepotism: "The arena of ambition had now become to me a ring where men are devoured by the beast-in-man after hideous battles" (247-48).

Sayler becomes Boss of the Power Trust, where money is regarded only as a serviceable commodity for buying vast and dramatic political favors. Granby, an adversary ruined by Sayler, commits suicide ("Something—like a scarecrow, but not a scarecrow—swung from a limb.... The face was distorted and swollen; the arms and legs drawn up in sickening crookedness" [288]); he had indicted Senator Sayler by an incriminating note. But the accused lawmaker has reached the respectable top; no one pays attention to the suicide letter; and Sayler is able to make a weakling, one Burbank, President—"my President" (295).

Harvey's wife conveniently dies of heart disease, and, now weary of the combative life in the savage political arena, he finds his way back to patient Elizabeth Crosby: "In me—in every one ... there's a beast and a man. Just now—with me—the man is uppermost. And he wants to stay uppermost. Elizabeth—will you—help him?" (389). She will: "I felt the full glory of those eyes, the full melody of that deep voice."

Harvey Sayler, as ambivalent in philosophy as the author who created him, is fundamentally a Darwinian with the drives and attitudes of the primitive: "My paths have not always been straight and open ...; like all others who have won in the conditions of this world of man still thrall to the brute, I have had to use the code of the jungle. In climbing I have had to stoop, at times to crawl. But, now ... I shall stand erect. I shall show that the sordidness of the struggle has not unfitted me to use the victory" (296). Simultaneously he is capable of feeling an honest emotional involvement with and commitment to "the cry of suffering humanity": "There was a time when I despised incapables; then I pitied them; but latterly I have felt for them the sympathetic sense of brotherhood. Are we not all incapables? Differing only in degree, and how slightly there, if we look at ourselves without vanity; like practice-sketches put upon the slate by Nature's learning hand and impatiently sponged away" (332).

Living "in the gladiatorial show called Life" (85), Sayler reflects the attitude of simple expediency and, perhaps knavishly, comes to a perception of the very close kinship between integrity and depravity, an affinity that had been sharply suggested two hundred years earlier by Bernard Mandeville in *The Grumbling Hive: or, Knaves Turn'd Honest* (1705):

> Thus every part was full of vice,
> Yet the whole mass a paradise;
> Flatter'd in peace, and fear'd in wars
> They were th' esteem of foreigners,
> And lavish of their wealth and lives,
> The balance of all other hives.
> Such were the blessings of that state;
> Their crimes conspir'd to make them great:
> And virtue, who from politics
> Has learn'd a thousand cunning tricks,
> Was, by their happy influence,
> Made friends with vice: And ever since,
> The worst of all the multitude
> Did something for the common good.[8]

Sayler, the political Svengali, made Burbank President; and the "presidency . . . made him a man" (293); Harvey offered to make "Doc" Woodruff, his crony with a criminal past, a senator. The moved Woodruff can only say "in a quiet earnest voice" that he has now been given "self-respect" (295). Thus Sayler easily discovers in himself the materials that can be rationalized into a life well and usefully spent: in a universe propelled by the immutable laws of chance, man can be an irresponsible agent; in a social contract motivated by acquisitive instinct and barbarous cruelty, he can do little else than help others to self-respect. Scarborough's moral perfectionism, then (". . . all evil passes. The good will be reaped." [385]), is ultimately made to face the amoralism of Sayler, who never experiences a "spasm of virtue." Like Mandeville, his Augustan predecessor in social philosophizing, Phillips has ascribed to Harvey Sayler the expedient, analytical strands embroidered in the "Moral" to "The Grumbling Hive":

> ... fools only strive
> To make a great and honest hive.
> T' enjoy the world's conveniences,
> Be famed in war, yet live in ease,
> Without great vices is a vain
> Eutopia seated in the brain.
> Fraud, luxury, and pride must live....[9]

To balance brutish vice with a tempering of justice and sentiment was the sum of Harvey Sayler's haphazard existence in the cesspool of American politics. His position at the close of the story is that of a statesman grown weary with power and tired of dispensing his largesse. Scarborough was above the common in the absolute purity of his uncompromising honor; Sayler was, to be sure, a Plunkitt of Tammany Hall, who opposed reformers, who believed in reciprocal patronage, and who felt that "Bosses Preserve the Nation."[10]

The Plum Tree had "considerable vogue"[11] and made for a literary parlor game; namely, trying to identify the originals of the characters the author had created. Doubtless Beveridge was Scarborough, although some nominated William Jennings Bryan for this honor; Senator Mark Hanna was the dubious nominee for Harvey Sayler's post, and William McKinley was suggested as Burbank.[12] Phillips never told his full intention; it seems evident that an amalgamation of these political personages was utilized. It is true, though, that the loving care lavished on Scarborough would lead one to Beveridge as the incontrovertible source.

The *Critic* called *The Plum Tree* Phillips' best novel, although its reviewer was not satisfied with the portrait of women in the tale;[13] but Flower's *Arena* beat the drum loud and strong: "It is in our judgment far and away the most important novel of recent years, because it unmasks present political conditions in a manner so graphic, so convincing and so compelling that it cannot fail to arouse the thoughtful to the deadly peril which confronts our people."[14] The novel is not a reformist tract, however, as is suggested by this review; exploration of Sayler is done with sympathy; one might even conclude that common sense would dictate every man's following Sayler's path, given his chemistry and opportunity.

One critic of *The Plum Tree*, a legislator well schooled in politics, castigated Phillips severely: in a personal letter from the White House, Theodore Roosevelt expressed his feelings on Phillips' political side-show to George Horace Lorimer. Dated May 12, 1906, the lengthy critique began with the President's confession that only Lorimer's warm suggestion prompted him to finish a book he had earlier thrown "aside after having gotten halfway through it."[15] Motivation for this anger came from what Roosevelt perceived was Phillips' "bitter contempt for the American democracy and its servants"[16] and the aroused President then chronicled with animated rhetoric the errors of the novelist: Phillips is "guilty" of "overstatement"; his "perspective" is "mistaken"; he "errs in making his big politicians think only of that which is directly to their own pecuniary interest"; and while "almost each individual fact brought forward by Phillips is true by itself ... these facts are so grouped as to produce a totally false impression." Most objectionable to Roosevelt, however, was the facile correlation in *The Plum Tree* of wealth with avaricious evil: "But to my mind the worst mistake that Phillips fell into—a mistake which has naturally resulted in his since enlisting under the banner of Hearst—was the mistake of painting all evil as due to corrupt commercialism, and all rich men as influenced only by what was base." There are "incendiaries, corruptionists, blackmailers, bribe takers" at all levels of the social collision of the day: "So it is wrong," asserted T. R., "to portray all men of capital as Mr. Phillips portrays them."

All elements mustered for the attack from the White House dealt, apparently, with Phillips' political judgment and with his manifest ignorance of the true internal functioning of national politics. Roosevelt intimated that the author was trying to project the local ward scramble on the screen of national scope where blemishes of the spirit are not so easily hidden. T. R. did not venture a criticism of the novel as a work of art, though he did make a comparison with Henry Adams' "sinister little novel called *Democracy*" as emanating from the same nefarious impulse as Phillips' unfortunate screed. Yet, the aroused broad-side which came from Roosevelt at *The Plum Tree* would later appear as gentle approbation when compared with White House reaction to *The Treason of the Senate*. David Graham Phillips, however, was not yet finished with his portraits of politics, plutocracy, and partisanship. With an eye on the career of flamboyant Thomas W. Lawson, he penned *The Deluge,* a novel called by the *Bookman* "his strongest. . . ."[17]

IV The Deluge

The ink was hardly dry on the first installment of Thomas Lawson's *Frenzied Finance: The Story of Amalgamated* in *Everybody's,* for July, 1904, when Phillips, following the trail of this timely *cause célèbre*, was composing the history of Matt Blacklock in *The Deluge* (1905). Before insider Lawson's astounding revelations of corporate procedure among the trusts and interlocking directorates was circulated across the country in *Everybody's,* he had gained a marginal reputation as "a daring and eccentric operator in the stock market"[18] as well as a suc-cessful business promoter, erratic sportsman, and imaginative impresario. Lawson, to his chagrin, was forever kept on the out-skirts of polite society (he was not admitted to membership in the New York Yacht Club) and was, at length, allegedly defrauded by his colleagues in capital. Having been an in-dependent operator, Lawson long was suspected of incipient treachery by those combines with whom he had become affili-ated; Standard Oil, in particular, was fearful lest this popular personality turn his strong public following against "The System." Actually, from the time he ran the Rand-Avery Press in Boston at the very start of his career in the late 1880's Law-son displayed a remarkable ability to attract people with his easy geniality and, at the same time, to arouse savage public fury.[19]

When his plutocratic colleagues marked him for economic oblivion, Lawson took his grievances to the people by publishing "disclosures of reckless viciousness" in American capitalism that brought to light "new capacities in the human spirit for the cruel and the avaricious."[20] From the inside of "The System,"

Thomas W. Lawson was able to present a vivid, electrifying picture of its cyclopean abuses:

> The everyday people, the millions who do not know Wall Street . . . lined with huge money-mills, where hearts and souls are ground into gold dust, whose gutters run full to overflowing with strangled, mangled, sandbagged wrecks of human hopes which, in a never-ending stream, it pours into the brimming waters of the river at its foot for deposit at the poorhouses, insane asylums, states' prisons, and suicides' graves. . . .[21]

From the character and exploits of frenzied Tom Lawson, Phillips fashioned his tale of "Black Matt" Blacklock, of whom one industrial titan in the novel shrewdly observed: "I have felt for two years . . . that Blacklock was about the most dangerous fellow in the country. The first time I set eyes on him, I saw he was a born iconoclast. And I've known . . . that some day he would use that engine of publicity of his to cannonade the foundations of society" (416).

The Deluge is the most successful of Phillips' works dealing with the American socioeconomic crises of the day because this material suited his timely sense of journalese and because the financial collision depicted was between diverse agents of *wealth alone*—an impersonal combine run by the plutocratic "Seven" and an affluent individual with a sense of honesty. Phillips made Blacklock inhabit the jungle of determinism but with a capable awareness not only of his dangers but also of his responsibility to those less fortunate in their endowments for struggle and survival. The tale in fact hinges on Blacklock's quick conversion to righteousness and a rapid development of his social consciousness to act as emotional catalyst against "The Seven" financiers set on ruining him.

This headlong clash of force runs concurrently with Blacklock's alternately sad and ecstatic marriage to Anita Ellersly, a woman of "superior fineness and breeding," whose feelings for her husband travel from "ice-like" revulsion at his crudeness to "burning" love for his honesty. For Blacklock is a "loner" on Wall Street, one who operates in an independent and unorthodox, however successful, manner: "How had I built up my power? By recognizing the possibilities of publicity, the chance which the broadcast sowing of newspapers and magazines put within the reach of the individual man. . . . The kings of finance relied upon . . . sundry paid agents. . . . I relied upon myself. . . . I spoke directly to the people" (5-6).

And it is a paradoxical "black" champion that we continue to see evolve in this bucket-shop trustee; for, through his eyes, we regard the polluted machinations of Roebuck, a "white-haired old scoundrel," the Bible-quoting nabob of "The System": "When my organization of the iron industry proved such a great success, and God rewarded my labors with large returns . . . I looked about me to see what new work He wished me to undertake, how He wished me to invest His profits" (112). And to explain a lockout according to the Gospel of Wealth: "Roebuck has been commanded by his God . . . to eject the free American labor from the coal regions and to substitute importations of coolie Huns and Bohemians. Thus, the wicked American laborers will be chastened for trying to get higher wages and cut down a pious man's dividends . . ." (341).

Blacklock, the narrator, observes that Roebuck and "his gang of so-called 'organizers of industry' bear about the same relation to industry that the boll weevil bears to the cotton crop" (124). Matt's outrage and indignation at the despoiling techniques and at the harvest of suffering reaped by Roebuck's unhappy victims break loose in the impulsive rhetoric of *j'accuse*: "Murder for dividends. Poison for dividends. Starve and freeze and maim for dividends. Drive parents to suicide, and sons and daughters to crime and prostitution for dividends. Not fair competition . . . but cheating and swindling, lying and pilfering and bribing, so that the honest and the decent go down before the dishonest and the depraved" (391).

An uneasy truce, a watchful toleration is established between Roebuck, his satellites, and Blacklock; for "Black Matt" has both wealth and influence, and the pious financial brigands, who admire his "pluck and impudence," occasionally "like to see fellows kick their way up among us from the common people" (472). When these nefarious "treasurers of the Lord" plan to ruin Blacklock, he begins to syndicate nationally a "History of the Industrial National Bank"; he opens fire on insurance spoliation and publicly holds up for inspection, one by one, "The Seven" master marauders of American dollars, property, and people. Following the conspicuous trail of Tom Lawson, Blacklock, with his accurate personal file of information on the trust manipulators, excoriates these evil "dabblers [in] slime of sordidness and snobbishness" (434).

His articles and newspaper advertisements precipitate "Wild Week," a panic of the "common man," when multitudes of the engulfed and the doomed little speculators storm the financial center. Because of their rage and fear, the sober words of Blacklock in the morning papers urging a new "leadership [under] the honest men of property" (454) are unheeded. His "friends," the people, turn on him: "Blacklock is responsible! . . . See the results of his crusade! He ought to be pilloried!" (459). As a discouraged Black Matt laments: "The people had risen for financial and industrial freedom; they had paid its fearful price; then, in senseless panic and terror, they flung it away" (460). With regrouped forces, the "luxurious army" and its crawling coterie of "parasites" take control once again. Matthew Blacklock remains a "loner," cast out by the plutocrats, rejected by the plebeians.

With Lawson's revelations of business life among the mass plunderers of society still running in *Everybody's* "when *The Deluge* left the press,"[22] it is difficult to understand a viewpoint of the *Outlook* which regarded the novel as "a readable story" but deplored "its extravagance [which] deprives it of any claim to be taken seriously."[23] If *The Deluge* has any merit, it derives from its fictional veracity, from the fact that "the incidents described, the characters portrayed . . . *were essentially true*."[24]

When the novelist departs from the realm of securities, wizardry, or Wall Street jugular infighting, the love tale takes precedence and plummets the tale to subterranean shoals of mawkish romance: "I took from my pocket the picture of Anita I always carried. 'Are *you* like that?' I demanded of it. And it seemed to answer: 'Yes—I am.' Did I tear the picture up? No. I kissed it as if it were the magnetic reality. 'I don't care what you are!' I cried. 'I want you! I want you!' " (435).

Apart from the exploits of a fictional Lawson and his romantic love story, Phillips forces the reader to contend with his propensity for *sententiae*, which seem to proliferate in *The Deluge* more than in his other novels: "Love means generosity, not greediness" (405); "Financiers do not gamble. Their only vice is grand larceny" (174); "Dirt looks worse in the midst of finery than where one naturally expects to find it—looks worse, and is worse" (97); "You can't establish a railway or a great industrial system by rose-water morality" (124). Moreover, the reader must also cut through some of Phillips' most pedestrian social philosophizing on "snobbery" and "human nature": "The wholesale merchant looks down on the retailer, the big retailer on the little; the burglar despises the pickpocket; the financier, the small promoter . . ." (54).

What remains of value in *The Deluge,* then, is the ability of Phillips to capture and preserve the enigmatic, untamed desperado Blacklock, a "master rogue" in the sense that James Galloway never was. Roebuck and his band of pious pirates appear as a flock of ancient, staid nobles suddenly scattered by a reckless scapegrace in a wild series of comic involutions. Certainly the fact that *The Deluge* is a fictionalized "case-study" does not dictate its necessary reality or value as history; the entire action can easily be visualized in a mythical area populated by the puppetry of the author; for the love tale is as scrupulously unreal as is the career in finance of the protagonist. Yet the entire era of the rise of bigness—the perpetrators of the varied gospels of wealth, greed, self-respect, and self-mastery— was a hurly-burly montage of the incredible, a "dollar hydrophobia" as Tom Lawson termed the *mal du temps.* Against the backgrounds of 26 Broadway, the headquarters of Standard Oil, and the marginal collusion that was characteristic of those diseased days, Phillips has frozen in time and space a portrait of Blacklock, a baron with mixed motives who captivates the reader as the frontier gambler-hero in the same tradition as John Oakhurst, Bret Harte's well-known martyr of Poker Flat. The uncontrollable elements in both stories are finally triumphant: Oakhurst commits suicide with the gesture of a Western folk-hero; Blacklock lives to fight another day, much to the fright of his nervous adversaries in profit manipulation.

David Graham Phillips had pushed on behind the newspaper headlines until the past had at this time caught up with him. From a generalized picture of a "master rogue," he had come to paint a rather genuine portrait of the actual rise and fall of such a type. He had explored in fiction the canyons of political corruption and its association with the "promoters of civilization"; he had examined the political superstructure of the country from ward heeler to President, from the unpaved streets of St. X, Indiana, to Pennsylvania Avenue. From both sides of the desk he had portrayed in his novels the rise of the mogul, his essential corruption, his depredation of the American public. With *The Deluge,* Phillips' documentary history of his times reached the fictional apex. His novels after *The Deluge* would no longer be able to stand as literary watchdogs of the social welfare. His interests in fiction were about to shift.

But first, having been led for a time by the headlines, Phillips was about to take a step that would cast himself and his work into the headlines themselves. He now wrote *The Treason of the Senate* for William Randolph Hearst's *Cosmopolitan* magazine; and, while recent commentators have praised these articles as "the high point in muckraking,"[25] their contemporary reception singled Phillips out as an irresponsible journalist whose lack of professional scruples could well put a sudden stop to the "literature of exposure."[26] His success with the formularized novels of business romance then in fashion failed to insulate Phillips from newspaper abuse of such virulence that the current of his future fiction would be altered completely.

CHAPTER 5

Stratagems and Spoils

THE IDEA of exposing the United States Senate did not originate in the mind of David Graham Phillips. Charles Edward Russell attributes inception of the plan for this unprecedented disclosure to himself; the final motivation came to him one day early in 1905 as he sat in the gallery of the Senate observing the "well-fed and portly gentlemen, every one of whom, we knew perfectly well, was there to represent some private (and predatory) Interest."[1] He sold the idea to the impulsive American newspaper magnate, William Randolph Hearst, who had only recently purchased *Cosmopolitan* and was looking for a gimmick to attract attention to the magazine. When *Everybody's* suddenly dispatched Russell on an assignment taking him around the world to research a series of articles on Populist movements abroad, he stopped work on gathering material for studies of the Senate and left the plan, still Hearst property, hanging fire.

To Bailey Millard, editor of *Cosmopolitan* and former editor of Hearst's San Francisco *Examiner,* fell the task of completing this promising assault on political privilege. Some believe that Millard himself had originated the idea of exposing the "house of dollars"; it is reasonably clear that he "came upon" the flashy title and made a direct offer to Phillips to complete Russell's job.[2] Phillips refused. He was furiously writing fiction; he was finished with articles; he could not afford the time. He suggested that Millard contact William Allen White. When White refused "on the grounds of lack of time," so the story goes, Millard turned again to Phillips, who wrote to the editor of *Cosmopolitan* on December 3, 1905, that he was apparently thinking it over: "As to the Senate series I don't know what to say. I'm so tied up for the next few months that I don't see how I can do it.

The subject is a good one and would attract attention. But the work would be exclusive of all my other work and would require a great deal of toiling terribly."³

At length Phillips, anxious to terminate the unlikely negotiations, named a "prohibitory" price, which, to his surprise, was met. Assistants were supplied: the author's brother William Harrison Phillips, a newspaperman, and Gustavus Meyers, who would soon publish *The History of Great American Fortunes* and who specialized in "original historical research."⁴ The project moved quickly forward. In February, 1906, *Cosmopolitan,* in an editorial foreword entitled "The Treason of the Senate," made this announcement with impudent fanfare:

> ... it should be the duty of every citizen of this republic—every man, woman, schoolboy and schoolgirl—every person who can understand facts as presented in print—to read ... a series of tremendously important articles to be commenced in the March number of the *Cosmopolitan.* A searching and unsparing spotlight, directed by the masterly hand of Mr. Phillips, will be turned upon each of the iniquitous figures that walk the Senate stage at the national Capitol. This convincing story of revelation ... is a ... terrible arraignment of those who, sitting in the seats of the mighty at Washington, have betrayed the public to that cruel and vicious Spirit of Mammon which has come to dominate the nation. ... Who is to protect us from the Senate? ... Who, then, is to protect the people but the press?⁵

On February 15, 1906, the March issue of *Cosmopolitan* was published. Through November of that year the American public was thereupon treated to a belaboring of "The Rich Man's Club" of undesirable statesmen in "the most vascular and virile"⁶ journalese the muckrakers had yet unearthed.

I *"The Treason of the Senate"*

The first installment of "Treason" unmasked the character of Chauncey Mitchell Depew of New York, the "railroad" senator whose duty it was "to serve his master, the plutocracy, in his old age as he [had] served it from his earliest youth"; he was "owned," so Phillips ardently declared, by Commodore Vanderbilt: "The Vanderbilts, when he entered their service, were engaged in stealing a series of franchises and existing railroads, and in getting upon the statute books laws legalizing the thefts and other laws making them absolute masters of the railway situation in the richest territory between New York and Buffalo. Their job was twofold—to rob the people and to rob the capitalists whom they had induced to invest in the stolen railways."[7]

Depew, Phillips asserts, has "the Archetypal Face of the Sleek, Self-satisfied American Opportunist in Politics and Plunder": "Treason is a strong word, but not too strong, rather too weak, to characterize the situation in which the Senate is the eager, resourceful, indefatigable agent of interests as hostile to the American people as any invading army could be, and vastly more dangerous; interests that manipulate the prosperity produced by all, so that it heaps up riches for the few; interests whose growth and power can only mean the degradation of the people, of the uneducated into sycophants, of the masses toward serfdom."[8] This Vanderbilt "butler," who was rewarded with "scant and contemptuous crumbs," maintained three majestic residences which *Cosmopolitan* photographed especially for the series, including a snapshot of the gilded, ornate drawing-room of the Depew palace in Washington.

Indeed, the unfortunate senator had the ill-fated luck to be lead subject for the glitter and flash of Phillips' biting prose and saw himself verbally mutilated in libelous proportions: "Depew . . . the sly courtier-agent, with the greasy conscience and the greasy tongue and the greasy backbone and the greasy hinges of the knees. . . . His nature was essentially servile, parasitic, typical of the truckler and the procurer."[9]

Phillips' impassioned onslaught against "Our Chauncey" even disturbed William Randolph Hearst when he read the article in proof, for he immediately fired off a telegram to George d'Utassy, his general manager, ordering more factual data to buttress the vehement arguments: "Violence is not force. Windy vituperation is not convincing. I had intended an exposé. We merely have an attack. The facts, the proof, the documentary evidence are an important thing, but the article is deficient in them."[10] The appearance of the article was delayed for a month (hence, an apologia in the February issue) while researchers supplied, to Phillips' delight and satisfaction, letters and testi-

mony from the official public transcript of the Insurance Investigating Committee. The frenzied writer thought the chapter on
Depew "a great improvement" with the new data.[11]

In April it was the turn of Senator Nelson W. Aldrich of
Rhode Island, "the right arm" of treason and "chief servant of
the Money Power in the Senate," to be run through the
Cosmopolitan gauntlet. This slave of "The Interests," whose
allegiance belonged to John D. Rockefeller, was designated as
the "permanent and undisputed boss" of the Senate, whose
"reverence for the Constitution" has legislated "more than half of
all the wealth created by the American people" into the hands
of "less than one per cent."[12] This dignified lawmaker, too, is
part of those "scurvy" gospellers "with their smirking and
cringing and voluble palaver about God and patriotism."

Nor is Aldrich exceeded in duplicity by Senator Arthur Pue
Gorman of Maryland, the May celebrity, who was charged as
"Left Arm of the Monster" and "shepherd" of "The Merger," that
Republican–Democrat coalition giving special attention to any
bill sponsored by "The Interests." He is expert in the "crafty,
treacherous ways of smothering, of emasculating, of perverting
legislation." While his major loyalty has been to the Sugar
Trust, Gorman is forever poised to "drive with expert hand a
knife into [the] heart" of legislation the "Interests" want killed,
as "Aldrich closes expert fingers on its throat to prevent outcry."[13]

In subsequent chapters Phillips examined Senator John C.
Spooner of Wisconsin, fluent "orator" for "The Interests" and
"spokesman of the merger";[14] Philander Chase Knox of Pennsylvania, who disported a record of "conspicuous devotion to the
men who exploit the labor and capital of the American people";[15]
Joseph Benson Foraker of Ohio, "whose record shows no act of
friendship or even neutrality toward the people in their struggle
with 'The Interests' ";[16] and Henry Cabot Lodge of Massachu-
setts, "respectable" outwardly but a sachem "who is the familiar
coarse type of machine politician, disguised by the robe of the
'Gentleman Scholar.' "[17]

Congress, both by its effected statutes and its failures to enact
needed laws, has made America a polluted grab-bag for the
few: "[Since] ... its failures to legislate against them [The
Interests] have not been frank and open but tricky, stealthy and
underhanded, the Senate cannot plead in its own defense either

ignorance or honest motives. . . ."[18] While Phillips seldom in the series approached the sustained invective he liberally had heaped upon "soul-vassal" Depew, to the very end he managed to keep his blunderbuss in scoring focus on the "treacherous Senate" and its club of conscientiously devoted plutocrats. *Cosmopolitan,* month after month, was sold out, and one jubilant patron echoed a popular sentiment of the day: "You have found a David who is able and willing to attack this Goliath of a Senate."[19] Perhaps the enterprising journal had found a verbal Goliath, but despite Hearst's "public-spiritedness" in sponsoring these awakening articles—plus a series on child labor by Edwin Markham that began in September of the same year—he was unable to find his much-coveted key to the State House in Albany; for on Election Day, 1906, Charles Evans Hughes defeated the magazine mogul in the New York gubernatorial race. Hearst's stepping-stone to the Presidency had eluded him.

II *The Muckraker and the President*

But much excitement was being generated by David Graham Phillips and his "Treason" articles. Letters of commendation poured in to the author from all over America,[20] and many writers expressed monumental delight with his attacks "on the Senatorial Brotherhood of Bankers' Footmen."[21] Yet the bellow unleashed against Phillips, his series, and Muckrakers generally, was so loud and emanated from such high quarters that the literature of reform was all but crushed lifeless. That Phillips was a political tool and toady was strongly hinted by the *Literary Digest* when, immediately after Senator Aldrich's moment in "the limelight of exposure," it slyly observed: "The *Cosmopolitan* is owned, be it said, by Congressman William Randolph Hearst (Dem.)."[22] In *Collier's Weekly,* cartoonist E. W. Kemble sketched "Our National Sport": Hearst and other magnates of the press at a fair throwing bricks at variously labeled heads (The Senate, Beef Trust, Standard Oil) peeping through a huge canvas that advertised to prospective customers, "Take a shy at the heads and increase your circulation."[23] Thus sporadic reaction to Phillips' public service was mixed, and, apparently for the major part, affirmative in terms of popular support from the rank-and-file magazine reading public.

When, however, on April 14, 1906, Theodore Roosevelt flexed his powerful presidential muscles with his address "The Man with the Muck-Rake," a speech "shot chiefly at Phillips,"[24] it became fashionable journalism to pillory those writers who had so recently been wielding the cudgels themselves. Phillips found himself a marked man and an unwitting accomplice in reform; his compatriots in the stocks were generally men with whom he had little sympathy, for he wished now to be considered primarily a novelist with a bent toward the timely and a sympathy for the despoiled. Roosevelt's "Muck-rake" speech succeeded in traumatizing Phillips, who, thoroughly confused, was grouped with the men of conscience, the impractical visionaries of reformism for whom he, a "sensible" operator, had little feeling.

Roosevelt's speech rallied the anti-muckrake forces as effectively as Emerson's *Divinity School Address* had sounded for Boston intellectuals the call to revolt against the "pale negations" of his contemporary Unitarianism. The President stressed in his address violent antipathy toward prodigal, indiscriminate assaults on men in public life; he thundered that "Hysterical sensationalism is the very poorest weapon wherewith to fight for everlasting righteousness,"[25] and that "There is mighty little good in a mere spasm of reform [for] violent emotionalism leads to exhaustion."[26] The stinging assault of the popular President could do nothing but undermine the confidence of the public in writers who remain so engrossed in "the filth of the floor" that they fail to regard for even an instant the "celestial crown":

> Now, it is very necessary that we should not flinch from seeing what is vile and debasing. ... But the man who never does anything else, who never thinks or speaks or writes save of his feats with the muck-rake, speedily becomes, not a help to society, not an incitement to good, but one of the most potent forces for evil ... I hail as a benefactor every writer or speaker, every man who, on the platform, or in book, magazine, or newspaper, with merciless severity makes such attack, provided always that he in his turn remembers that the attack is of use only if it is absolutely truthful. The liar is no whit better than the thief, and if his mendacity takes the form of slander, he may be worse than most thieves. It puts a premium upon knavery untruthfully to attack an honest man, or even with hysterical exaggeration to

assail a bad man with untruth. An epidemic of indiscriminate
assault upon character does not good, but very great harm. The
soul of every scoundrel is gladdened whenever an honest man
is assailed. . . .[27]

Roosevelt denounced the "excess," the "gross and reckless" tone
of assassinations in print, and "the morbid and vicious public
sentiment" thereby aroused. With the president's closing words
"about clean living and right thinking," the era of what Lincoln
Steffens called "journalistic investigations" abruptly came to
a halt.

The day following his speech Roosevelt explained to Steffens
that "He had been aroused by an article on 'poor old Chauncey
Depew by David Graham Phillips' " and that he spoke out
mainly to offer solace to the beleaguered senator who had been
"painted as a traitor."[28] A more explicit and fundamental animus,
however, was reflected in a letter of May 23, 1906, when T. R.
wrote to George Horace Lorimer: "I do not believe that the
articles that Mr. Phillips has written, and notably these articles
on the Senate, do anything but harm. They contain so much
more falsehood than truth that they give no accurate guide
for those who are really anxious to war against corruption, and
they do excite a hysterical and ignorant feeling against everything existing, good or bad. . . .[29]

In this letter which the President labeled "Personal and
Private," he excoriated Phillips as "a foul-mouthed coarse black-
guard" who "certainly makes no serious effort to find out the
facts" and who "is guilty of reckless untruth." Roosevelt unleashed an angry barrage of bitterness that must have startled
Lorimer, Phillips' good friend, by its rancor and ferocity:

> You say that Phillips himself is an absolutely straight and
> honest man. . . . I can only avoid questioning it by unstintedly
> condemning his judgment and his diligence. You doubtlessly
> know that many entirely honest people firmly believe that Mr.
> Phillips in accepting the money of Mr. Hearst to attack the
> public servants of the United States, was actuated merely by a
> desire to achieve notoriety and at the same time to make money
> out of the slanders. . . . To be in the employ of Mr. Hearst and
> engaged in such work as Mr. Phillips is engaged in, from the
> point of view of ethics, is not one particle better than to be a
> public man engaged in the practices he rightly condemns.[30]

In view of Lorimer's friendship with both Beveridge and the bespattered muckraker, it is no doubt true that Phillips saw the letter or at least was made aware of its contents. Yet, even if he never learned of the President's sentiments, the number of attacks against Phillips and the journalist-reformers which now came pouring from the press only intensified the sad realization that he had done poorly to forsake fiction and worse to be pushed into the quicksand of unpopular reformism. In January, 1907, Roosevelt and Phillips met at the Gridiron Club; the President wrote Beveridge: "I must confess that I was extremely pleased to meet Phillips and took a fancy to him. I thoroly [*sic*] understand your having stood by him."[31] Still, President Roosevelt maintained a suspicious distrust of all muckrakers, even "the more honest ones."[32]

In the wake of Roosevelt's speech came a wave of brutal reaction against the "soldiers of the common rake." The Chicago *Evening Post* praised the President for "deodorizing and disinfecting such compost heaps as the man with the muck-rake gathers,"[33] while the New York *Sun* gloated over the obsequies of the group: "It was a great day while it lasted, but it became too hot. The Muck-rakers worked merrily for a time in their own bright sunshine, and an unthinking populace applauded their performance. Now there are few to do them reverence."[34]

In an address delivered before the American Periodical Publishers' Association, Ex-President Grover Cleveland sought a "force to balance the impetuosity and check the recklessness which are [*sic*] apt to grow out of the existing havoc of overturning,"[35] and W. D. Nesbit in the New York *Times*, with apologies to Kipling, lampooned the reformers in poetic parody:

"What are the bugles blowing for?" said Lawson-on-Parade
"To turn us out, to turn us out," D. Graham Phillips said. . . .
They're exposin' the exposers; it would make your hair turn gray
To reflect on what will come when they expose each exposé,
When they find a newer frenzy or a treason every day—
They're exposin' the exposers in the mornin'.[36]

The Chicago *Tribune* heralded a "return of public sanity" and offered a considered evaluation of what killed the corruption hunters in American periodical literature:

Indeed, an interesting chapter in the book of graft would be one written by a converted muckraker relating the way in which he wove gossamer films of suspicion into a web resembling a solid structure, careless whether the first breath of truth would destroy it. Invective took the place of fact, half truths were made to seem damning where the whole truth would have been creditable. Ignorance attributed to questionable motives, actions which greater knowledge would have shown to be inevitable or salutary. Petty and irrelevant scandals . . . personal gossip . . . [and] sheer inventions of enemies, were all treated as if revelations of the most important character.[37]

With no endeavor to plumb the social or psychological ramifications of the matter, the Philadelphia *Press* plainly and succinctly noted that "People are sick of the muck-rake" and "a healthy reaction has begun."[38]

Still, a more forcible condemnation was directed at Phillips when "The Treason of the Senate" reached its serialized conclusion. *Collier's*, itself a popular repository of muckraking literature, singled out David Graham Phillips as an unscrupulous literary opportunist and juxtaposed his name with the roll of honest author-reformers:

"The Treason of the Senate" has come to a close. These articles made reform odious. They represented sensationalism and money-making preying on the vogue of the "literature of exposure," which had been built up by truthful and conscientious work of writers like Miss Tarbell, Lincoln Steffens and Ray Stannard Baker. . . . Mr. Phillips' articles were one shriek of accusations based on the distortion of such facts as were printed, and on the suppression of facts which were essential.[39]

If Phillips had maintained his composure and equanimity through the many and varied attacks from White House to town journal, under this final shock he was "far less stoical."[40] The *Collier's* attack left him literally reeling, and Charles Edward Russell reports that "I had an anxious time with him [Phillips] that Sunday, walking him around the streets while I tried to comfort and console him under the blow. He was terribly cut up. . . ."[41] An innocent half-hearted accomplice pressured into the arena of reform, he, alone, was branded "dishonest." The bleak irony of the situation failed to alleviate the depression that clouded over Phillips; the numerous "crank" and threatening letters he received could not have troubled his forthright consciousness more than this alleged venality of his broadcast in the press. As a result, he decided that he would effect a retreat from the magazines; he would return to his fiction and, as soon as he could dispatch prior literary commitments, sound a weary "farewell to reform."

Unlike many other tracts of the muckrakers, "The Treason of the Senate" was not dignified by publication as a book. Its startling, shocking contents were permitted to gather dust in the bound volumes of *Cosmopolitan* magazine in library basements. At last in 1954, as a historical curio, a slender collection was brought out for new generations of students, insulated by time from the bombast and furor that surrounded the month-by-month dissection of America's most infamous "misrepresentatives." The final contemporary footnote to *Treason* was supplied in 1962 by Upton Sinclair, himself a notorious muckraker at the very time Phillips was so controversial a journalist. Observed the eighty-four-year-old compatriot in reform: "The articles were basically sound, though I had the impression that Phillips, whom I knew rather well, was longer on adjectives than facts."[42]

III The Second Generation

The core of Phillips' interest now began to undergo a change. The abusive treatment to which he had been subjected argued for a turn to pastures new, and in a short time he was to discover his summit of interest by a passionate embrace of the social virus with which he had always been infected, "The New Woman," her rights, ideals, and dilemmas. In this period of literary transition he tried his hand at a fantasy with a broad base of sensible utopianism (paradox) in *The Second Generation* (1907), which had appeared serially in *Success* (March, 1906–January, 1907), and which reflects almost consciously Phillips' retreat into a world of simple, homey, Midwest virtues of honesty and calm self-sufficiency. Still, for all his pains to preach common sense to a public that obviously was now immune to hysterical prose, Phillips saw his book blistered as "Socialistic."[43] The *Arena,* again his critical ally, came to his psychic aid by claiming that "*The Second Generation* is not only Mr. Phillips's strongest and best novel; it is the most virile and vital romance of the present year."[44]

The novel deals with Hiram Ranger, "master workman," "manufacturing partner," and "controlling owner" of the Ranger–Whitney Company of Saint Christopher and Chicago—who is told by Dr. Schulze that he will soon die. This self-made capitalist must set his house in order. His son Arthur, a Harvard dilettante and "jay," along with his socially minded daughter Adelaide, must by custom be adequately, even handsomely, provided for in the father's will. Ranger, however, wants to avoid placing the curse of inherited wealth upon his weak, misadvised children; and, by leaving nearly all of his vast fortune to local Tecumseh Agricultural and Classical University, he consigns his heirs to an embarrassed, aristocratic poverty. Hiram Ranger feels that Arthur's manhood will be spared, for the disappointed collegian must now prove himself in Alger-like fashion by "starting at the bottom" and "learning the business."

The major theme of the tale involves Arthur and his gradually changing feelings toward the memory of his wise father: from anger and hatred at being "cut-off" and relegated to a standard of living the social misery of which young Ranger had never known, to wholehearted respect and admiration for the real legacy Hiram had bequeated to him: ".... Arthur Ranger is a credit to any father. He's becoming famous.... And he's respected, honest, able, with a wife that loves him. Would he have been anybody if his father had left him the money that would have compelled him to be a fool?"(314). Mark Hargrave, president of the university, gives voice to the ethical nucleus of the novel: "It is the curse of the world, this inherited wealth.... Because of it humanity moves in circles instead of forward. The ground gained by the toiling generations, is lost by the inheriting generations. And this accursed inheritance tempts men ever to long for and hope for that which they have not earned" (71). Phillips dramatizes this thesis, once again, with his sentimental romance. Arthur and his sister are socially ostracized by the "snobbish sets" who wallow in fashionable luxury; at last, he marries Madalene Schulze, doctor of medicine like her father; Adelaide marries Dory Hargrave, whose interest lies not in making money but in "Montaigne and Don Quixote, Shakespeare and Shelley and Swinburne" (332).

Minor financial scuffling sops up some narrative energy as Whitney, Sr., endeavors to wrest control of the Ranger industries, but what the critics startled at most involved a "revolutionary scheme" which the radical Arthur introduced, a plan which enabled Tecumseh University and the Ranger mills to operate as complementary organizations for the benefit of the "common workman." His "many foolish notions" became in the novel subjects for wide discussion: "You see, money is coined sweat. All its value comes from somebody's labor. He [Arthur] deserves to be rewarded for happening to have a better brain than most men, and for using it better. But there's no fund for rewarding the clever for being cleverer than most of their fellow-beings . . . So he has to choose between robbing his fellow-workmen, who are in his power, and going without riches. He prefers going without" (286-87).

The radicalism of Arthur Ranger, however, extended further as he encouraged, so townspeople declared, "the workmen to idleness": "He's going to establish a seven-hours' working day; and, if possible, cut it down to six." The fusion of the plant and the university inflamed St. X with a lethal passion. Madalene explained plans for adult and technical education: "And . . . the university is to change its schedules so that all its practical courses will be at hours when men working in the factory can take them. Its simply another development of his and Dory's idea that a factory belonging to a university ought to set a decent example—ought not to compel its men to work longer than is necessary for them to earn at honest wages a good living for themselves and their families" (287). Dividends will be abolished; all students will engage in productive labor on the university's farms, workshops, and factories. The entire educational operation will be self-supporting. There will in this society be abundant chance for self-perfection: "a human race that is really fine, really capable, [and] has a real standard of self-respect" (288).

Adelaide calls the experiment "a beautiful dream"; opponents roared out against this "hotbed of anarchy" with its total "concession to the working classes." For laborers at other plants in Saint X had "fixed tenaciously upon the central fact that the university's men worked . . . fewer hours each day by four to seven, and even eight, got higher wages, got more out of life in every way" (297). Arthur had substituted "the power of an intelligent public opinion" to induce his workmen "to live in tasteful comfort" and "to acquire sane habits"; he went beyond the generally employed "crafty, inexpensive schemes of benevolent charity" (297-98).

One can perceive the strategy behind Phillips' stern analysis of his society and his rather tenuous and glib prescription for its ills. He had been stung by "The Interests" and their organs of circulation. His bitterness gave expression to a world picture not particularly attractive to reviewers of *The Second Generation*:

> Mankind found this world a hell, and is trying to make it over into a heaven. And a hell it still is, even more of a hell than at first, and it'll be still more of a hell—for these machines and these slave-driving capitalists with their luxury-crazy families are worse than wars and aristocrats. . . . Some day the world'll be worth living in—probably just about the time it's going to drop into the sun. Meanwhile, it's a hell of a place. (168-69)

Clearly, a changed David Graham Phillips postulates this ardent speech in behalf of the Veblenism he had only a short time ago dismissed with belittling scorn. And his own reception was the cutting hostility accorded a new radical novelist. The *Independent* continued the assault that had begun on "Treason": "On the whole the book teaches us to be thankful that the social and industrial salvation of the country is not in the hands of these ingenious fiction makers, particularly those who have a socialistic heaven in view which none of us are fit by nature or grace to enter."[45]

William M. Payne, discussing *The Second Generation* in the *Dial*, dealt with the novel as art, in addition to pointing up the more disturbing elements of the theme: "Unfortunately, Mr. Phillips has no style, and thus his management of a strongly-conceived situation becomes bald and unconvincing. The moral of the story is so fine and true despite a slight tincture of unwholesome socialism, that we could wish the author's literary gift were more in proportion to his ethical insight."[46]

Despite his former claim to expertness in politics when the Pulitzer entourage had gathered for consultation, Phillips was an amateur dabbler in the drama of the political situation. When

he had in March, 1905, contributed to the *Arena* his study of
"The New School of Socialism in Europe," he had defined this
phenomenon as "...the brotherhood of man...the infamy of
war...[and] the community of goods."[47] He would choose
Socialism over the "imperial oligarchy" created by an "aristocracy
of wealth."[48] Yet the dynamics of Socialism either as a political
panacea or as an ideological creed held no interest for the
sensible, pragmatic Phillips as he violently swung from his
militant rugged individualism to a vision of Utopia—a Garden of
Eden that could be planted in a most uncomplicated manner. If
not through the seething cauldron of spectacular reform, perhaps
through the starry example of the Ranger family and Tecumseh
University could present-day man be given a vision of what the
future might hold for him. Phillips' publisher steered clear of
the controversial aspects of *The Second Generation* in promoting
the book, being content to note that "It has been called a
problem novel" and that the tale is handled in a "Balzacian
way."[49] Most appealing to prospective readers, however, was
its alluring designation as "a double-decked romance" of a
struggle for "love, happiness, and life."[50]

Phillips' future productions were not to prove politically
embarrassing to him. His "socialistic" phase was over. It had
endured through one book. A primordial tug at his intellect
perhaps had joggled Phillips' memory to his days at Princeton
and to his study of Gissing's *Demos*.

IV Light-Fingered Gentry

Phillips now returned for one final excursion into the timeliness of crusading reformism to recapture the easy source of
literary access he had earlier established in his novels of the
business world and its alliances with power, politics, and spoliation. *Light-Fingered Gentry* (1907), serialized in *Pearson's*
from September, 1906, to June, 1907, was based on the notorious
insurance scandals brought to light by one of Thomas Lawson's
assertions in *Everybody's* for December, 1904: "I am going to
cause a life insurance blaze...."[51] Popular journals gave prominent space to this eruption; Flower's *Arena* leaped into the
fight for insurance reform,[52] and *McClure's* in May, 1906, began
to serialize Burton J. Hendricks' "The Story of Life Insurance,"

an analysis of the gaming techniques and fraudulent people who characteristically generated the whirlpool of insurance spoils. In the *Independent* (December, 1906) Louis D. Brandeis had cried out against "The Great Life Insurance Wrong" by protesting that "The extraordinary wastefulness of the present system . . . is due in large part to the fact that the business, whether conducted by stock or by mutual companies, is carried on for the benefit of others than the policy holders."[53] He deplored that, "in the conduct of the business, the interests of the insured are ignored."

All New York followed the *World's* exposé of the "High Life Insurance" party given by James Hazen Hyde, incompetent playboy heir of Equitable, who squandered seventy-five to two-hundred thousand dollars of the policyholders' savings on the decadent affair.[54] Ironically, these companies were advertised as "the sacred trusts of widows and orphans" and with this slogan lobbied for special privileges; their directors were the supposed epitomes of respectability: eminent financiers and Congressmen. Said Lincoln Steffens: "I could pick crooks who would do better than those highly respectable business men."[55] Certainly so magnetic a chain of events could not be bypassed by David Graham Phillips, who novelized the corruption in insurance, cleaned it up, and painted a young vigorous Midwesterner first caught in the shackles of perfidy and theft, then rising to the rarified heights of honesty and philanthropy, bearing upward with him the aspirations and dreams of the small policyholders insured by the Mutual Association Against Old Age and Death, the O.A.D.

The original manuscript of *Light-Fingered Gentry* bore the title *The Story of Neva* [and Armstrong];[56] thus, the author's major concern was again with the personal relationship and entanglements of a couple rather than with scientific analysis and presentation of the insurance scandals in their tedious technical detail. The drama of insurance corruption, forms, therefore, the backdrop for another love tale that travels Phillips' limited gamut of emotional experience. Neva Carlin and Horace Armstrong of Battle Field, Indiana, are divorced; he goes to New York to become an executive with the O.A.D.; she later comes there to study painting with Boris Raphael, a well-known artist who becomes her suitor. Armstrong soon realizes that he is part of an "infamous conspiracy" and is regarded as the "unscrupulous henchman" of Josiah Fosdick, president of the firm which specializes in "robbing dead bodies [and] picking the pockets of calico mourning dresses" (241). Armstrong's position with this "philanthropic institution" comes to be "a puller-in for a den of respectable thieves" who are forever conniving to steal from widows and orphans: "Ours is the vilest trick of all. . . . For we play on peoples' heart strings, while the other swindles appeal chiefly to cupidity" (240-41). Pious Fosdick, however, has duped the public into believing that anyone "investigating" insurance conditions is a "plausible blackmailer" and a "disguised anarchist"; he righteously voices his outrage: ". . . the damn fool public has been liquored up with all sorts of brandy by reformers and anarchists and socialists, trying to set it on to tear down the social structure" (91).

The denouement easily comes about: Neva, who intuitively senses that Armstrong is involved in fiscal corruption, learns from a victim the real horrors of O.A.D.:

> "My father," replied the boy. "He died day before yesterday. And we had to have the money for the funeral. We're all insured to provide for that. And my mother went down to collect father's insurance. It was for a hundred and twenty-five dollars. We'd paid in a hundred and forty on the policy. . . . they told her they couldn't get it through and pay it for about three weeks—and she had to have the money right away. . . . they give her eighty-two dollars for the policy. . . . Only, they didn't give her cash. They gave her a credit with an undertaker—he's in cahoots too." (344)

With quiet pressure from Neva and with a reconciliation between them in the offing, Armstrong revolts against the "stewardship" of Fosdick and his hosts of gamblers, parasites, and grafters; he levels the O.A.D. and begins rebuilding the insurance firm on foundations of honesty and humanity. Armstrong will no longer be "a shearer" of downtrodden "sheep." He has met Neva's challenge to return to his high principles, and the couple will be reconciled.

There are two notable subsidiary themes in *Light-Fingered Gentry*: one deals with love and patriotism; the other, with evolution and force. Neva is given the choice of soft, sentimental

Raphael, the painter who begs for her love ("You make me tremble with passion and with fear" [375]) or of hard, practical Armstrong, who, as a vigorous American, deplores Neva's friendship with "that damned, scented foreigner, with his rings and his jewelled canes and his hand-kissing" (237). Boris Raphael lapses into French when he declares his love; he is, as Neva sees him, "too subtle, too nervous, too appreciative, too changeable" (374). When he realized that Neva loved Armstrong, the artist's angry appearance "suggested a dark Sicilian hate peering from an ambush, stiletto in impatient hand" (374). There is painted a certain sinister foreignism about Raphael that makes him direct foil to Armstrong, who finally is brought to realize that he must give up his part in insurance swindling because, as Neva tells him, "It isn't American—it isn't decent—it isn't brave" (402).

Phillips also promotes a direct picture of the universe as motivated by the evolutionary powers governed by brute force. Armstrong attempts to explain his complicity in insurance fraud by proclaiming: "I don't quibble; I act. I don't criticize life; I live. I don't create the world or make the law of the survival of the fittest; I simply accept conditions..." (403). The author himself makes a direct statement to the reader enforcing this philosophic version of the cosmos in which *Light-Fingered Gentry* was cast:

> Heart, and his younger brother, Mind, are two newcomers in a universe of force. They fare better than formerly; they will fare better hereafter; but they are still like infants exposed in the wilderness. Some fine natures have enough of the tough fiber successfully to make the fight; others, though they lack it, persist and prevail by chance—for the brute pressure of force is not malign; it crushes or spares at haphazard. (157)

Phillips' fictional *deus ex machina*, however, included a basic belief in a salutary force: a prevailing benevolent Power (not God) that invariably harnessed the brute and converted his prolific energy into a force for good. Horace Armstrong's career illustrates this thesis.

The timeliness of the novel in no way assisted it to a favorable press reception; in fact, this very feature evoked negative responses from the New York *Times*: "... as a whole it is the sort of novel which is . . . cousin to the special article of the monthly magazine and the work of the star reporter on the daily newspaper."[57] And the reviewer in the *Outlook* wrote: "The colors—the . . . yellow of the sensational journalist and the dismal black of the chronic pessimist—are laid on with a prodigal brush."[58] Once more, though, B. O. Flower and the *Arena* heaped great praise on Phillips for showing "the plutocracy at work in secret": "Now if they [the people] permit the criminal rich to continue to oppress through immoral business practices and the debauching of government, they become partners in the crime, abetters in a nation's destruction. . . . America's great Monte Carlo cannot continue as it has prospered during recent decades, and free institutions survive or the people escape the slavery of extortion, of remorseless greed."[59]

Again Phillips had followed hard on the heels of a transient phenomenon flitting across the stage of contemporary life. His literary reservoir, always rather low, had by now reached the sandy bottom. He now began to take up in his remaining works the theme that always had held a more than faint literary attraction for him: The New Woman. Indeed, almost as a conscious prelude to this shift of focus, Phillips had Horace Armstrong lash out at Neva: "You are of this new type—the woman that uses her brain. Give me the old-fashioned kind—the kind that loved, without question" (433).

CHAPTER 6

The Business of Being a Woman

WHEN HAROLD FREDERIC created Celia Madden, the Celtic beauty in *The Damnation of Theron Ware* (1896), he analyzed a personality whose unorthodox character would soon have appeal for David Graham Phillips: The New Woman, a phenomenon, Havelock Ellis had stated in 1891, that helped produce a spirit capable of vitalizing the "degenerate" culture of a *fin-de-siècle* world. Celia takes her freedom with outspoken seriousness:

> What on earth is it to me that other women crawl about on all-fours, and fawn like dogs on any hand that will buckle a collar onto them, and toss them the leavings of the table? I am not related to them. I have nothing to do with them. They cannot make any rules for me. If pride and dignity and independence are dead in them, why, so much the worse for them! It is no affair of mine. Certainly it is no reason why I should get down and grovel also. No; I at least stand erect on my legs.[1]

Celia, a daughter of wealth, could live, as she put it, by "whim"; on the other hand, even the newly emancipated woman was victimized at the time by a necessary economic dependence that Charlotte Perkins Stetson regarded as unethical and unjust: "The women who do the most work get the least money, and the women who have the most money do the least work."[2]

To understate the dilemma, women and economics formed a perplexing combination. Even the most sincere male reformers who stumped in behalf of the New Independent Woman seldom looked beyond a vision of the American female as an idealized, sentimental entity holding real, however vague, propensities for good and for uplifting the race through this veiled beneficence.

Charles Edward Russell phrased it thus: "... if the 'eternal feminine' should cease to lead us upward forever, if the idealism and loftier impulses that woman furnishes in the world, were to be crushed out of it, I cannot see wherein would lie the least chance for progress."[3] A "sob-sister" of 1908 sounded the theme in this manner: "... but let me tell you ... *no mission is nobler, or more far-reaching, than that of establishing the 'Little Kingdom of Home,' and becoming the mother in that home.* The woman who does this comes much closer to fulfilling her 'woman's mission' than her sister who remains a maid, however great her power of doing good."[4]

The Kingdom of Home, however, had been earlier made part of an awkward equation: women and horses, complained Mrs. Stetson, both inhabit the stable of economic dependence. Thus, when a dedicated social critic, as Russell assuredly was, insisted that "The industrial woman is here," his words were merely powerless cant. Anna A. Rogers knew very well the reasons for the synthetic discontent voiced by unhappy ladies: "American women constantly cry out against the smallness of their lives, the limitations that encompass them.... They cry out against certain social evils, and they forget that the ranks are ever recruited from among the daughters of Vanity, Uncontrol, and Idleness."[5] No class of woman was denounced more in newspaper and magazine during the first decade of the twentieth century than the "idle" woman, the "parasite." Even Mrs. Gabrielle E. Jackson, strong, unctuous advocate of the Kingdom of Home, was forced to chant, albeit in sweet falsetto: "And is there anything lovelier upon earth than the gentlewoman bread-winner? How one's heart goes out to her, how we respect and love her for her courage."[6]

Phillips, however, was not such a professional feminist. Always interested primarily in his fiction and anxious at this time to leave political arenas as sites for his novels, he focused his attention on the "Woman Problem" as a literary vehicle. No philosopher, no sociologist, and no reformer, Phillips began to exploit passion among the plutocrats until his fiction came to be encompassed by a Love Mystique that proliferated through popular magazines in their stories and advertising and in the daily newspapers in their editorials.

The newspaper kingdom of William Randolph Hearst circulated many a viewpoint on the "Woman Question" that came to stand as a basis for Phillips' polemical novels. Hearst and his editorial arm Arthur Brisbane attacked the "sentimental idea" of placid reverence for the "middle-aged lady" as "false." Their editorial campaigns were directed against the woman who *"gives up thinking early in life."* The reason given for such surrender was simple: "Many women suffer undoubtedly from the sentimental, physical and intellectual reaction caused by the cessation of the responsibility of maternity." And the lamentable conclusion was that "There are in the United States hundreds of thousands of splendid brains going to waste among our women, because they do not realize the duty of using, to the last, all the intellectual power within them."[7]

In "When Will Her Mental Power Begin?" the editor looked to the day when woman "will be able to cultivate her mind." At that time, "She will have more of a hold on Mr. Selfish Man, and he will have to pay more attention to her." Indeed, "the woman with the big brain" lives in a "happy home that needs no divorce lawyer";[8] but, while Hearst would direct the American Woman to paths of the intellect, he would also urge her to preserve vanity, a "useful" trait, *the one and indispensable preserver of her health.*[9] The generalizations comprising the entire editorial reveal a public picture of "the idle woman" busily involving herself in what Mrs. Rogers called "the rushing current" of contemporary life with its sordid emphasis on pleasurable delights of the palate: "A woman's instinct is to eat buckwheat cakes, adding boiling hot coffee and iced water. She likes to eat candy between meals, and her idea of a fine luncheon is lobster salad and ice cream. But small spots appear. Those fine pink cheeks get too pink or too pale...."[10]

Next are considered "hideous corset squeezing," "abominable cigarettes," and "stimulants to excess." The Vanity of womanhood, however, will steer her, in the long run, from this Roman self-indulgence. Certainly no lady proud of her appearance would tolerate such frightful disintegration as the Hearst editorial enumerates: "make the face sallow," "make the eyes heavy," "develop a mustache."[11] As an anonymous contributor to a symposium entitled "The American Woman and Her Home" noted in the *Outlook* for September, 1910: "Beauty is as necessary in man's environment as light. . . . Every woman owes to her family, to society, and to herself the sacred obligation to be a thing of beauty."[12]

The cult of the American Woman during the first decade of the twentieth century grew as each passing month brought more articles on various aspects of Feminism. Numerous commentators felt the need to contribute to a lore which nearly always managed to find its way into print—and frequently in the most antisocial, unscientific journals. Most interesting, captivating, and exotic, however, was the woman of what Elbert Hubbard called the "Superior Class," whose major charm and elegance was "Conspicuous Display"; in *The Philistine,* his "Periodical of Protest," Hubbard wrote:

> . . . men have delegated to women the task of Conspicuous Waste. The man supplies the materials—she does the rest. We now know a man's financial standing by the way his wife dresses. His wife is his walking rating in R. G. Dun & Co.'s register. . . . He works and toils and slaves with his head and wit—*not hands*—[italics mine] so as to buy seal-skin sacques, jewels, silks, laces, and princely carriages and a palace with many servants—all for his wife and daughters. It is a vicarious waste. . . .[13]

The "idle woman" of this class is symbol "of the power and potency" of her silk-shirted, white-collared husband who "by hook or crook, secures the labor of many men and women and also children"; who "has mills in various places"; and who "draws tribute from a thousand sources."[14] This type of American woman, so states Mrs. Newell Dwight Hillis, "consciously or unconsciously" spurs her husband on to greater acquisitiveness "until he falls, if not under the hand of a merciful Providence, under the stress of temptation."[15] Clearly, this social menace was regarded as a shallow, ego-driven, irresponsible sybarite.

The St. Louis *Mirror* of William Marion Reedy, nevertheless, upheld the morals of this woman: "It is all bosh to say that unfaithfulness prevails among society women. They are as faithful as the wives of the poor. Their position would enforce faithfulness, if their moral sense did not. They are observed. American society women are unromantic. One might almost proclaim their virtue upon the poor ground that their blood is snow-broth."[16] Brann, the Iconoclast, not convinced by this "mellow radiance of Arthurian romance," countered:

> . . . any kind of weather would indeed be dreary to the average society dame if she could not have a gallant or two traipsing at her heels. The society woman is indeed "observed." She is observed boating, bathing, biking, and strolling in leafy dells on moonless nights with noted "mashers," while her hubby is worrying thro' the summer in a distant city. She is observed at the opera, while her matrimonial mate is soaking his bunions at home—taking lunch with her escort afterwards; disporting herself at balls until late hours, then carried home in a closed carriage much the worse for wine. . . . Money covers a multitude of sins, and the woman of great wealth may have as many lovers as she likes without impairing her social position. . . .[17]

The belle of the fashionable set, then—the woman whose major problems were facing "the increase of luxury,"[18] indulging a "complacent egotism,"[19] and nourishing the "bacillus" for "social-climbing"—came to be a flourishing phenomenon on the American scene, recognized and analyzed by pedestrian and artist alike. Ethel Lloyd Patterson, however belatedly, noted in the New York *Evening World* of November 2, 1910, that "David Graham Phillips is interested in the American woman. He does not care for politics at all." More precisely, Phillips' interest in The New Woman had suddenly achieved a resolution; his kaleidoscopic, minor treatment of the "woman theme" in his earlier novels now appeared sharply in focus at the very core of his fiction. "The Treason of the Senate" had prompted numerous innuendos about Phillips' lack of dedication to truth; at this time, his honesty would be unquestionable, but he would come to be derided as an author unable to avoid "the pitfalls of vulgarity"[20] and "bad taste."[21]

I "Restless Husbands"

Phillips' ideas on "the American woman" represent in the main a pastiche of the fables, clichés, and prejudices of his day; but he made a scrupulous effort to unify coherently the various battlegrounds he perceived in the war of the sexes. He offered the essay "Restless Husbands" to George Horace Lorimer in

November, 1909, for $500,[22] but the editor probably felt that
Phillips' bitter sentiments might be too controversial for the
Saturday Evening Post. Thus, *Cosmopolitan* for August, 1911
(Phillips had been dead for more than six months), carried the
novelist's posthumous indictment of the American woman. His
attitudes were not shocking, for Phillips had chained The New
Woman to his literary pillory at least four years before the essay
was published. He had accused her of being somewhat more
than an accomplice in the moral and spiritual defection present
in the American male: he attributed to her sole responsibility
for "the rapidly widening gap" between the sexes in America.
Their "sympathies, tastes, [and] ideals" lay in opposite directions:
"Every foreigner who comes to inspect us is struck by it, is
amazed that the beautiful, graceful, utility-abhorring American
woman, aristocratic in all her ideas, should be able to get
along at all with the hard-working, common American man. He
sees a woman who is marrying into the foreign aristocracies;
who is striving to create, in the great toilsome American cities,
an aristocracy of idle playing-about; who abhors the American
gospel of work. . . ."[23]

Phillips then offers his classification of the various types of
destructive females presently populating America and subverting
its traditionally noble aims. Foremost is the "Parasite": "This
class is the new American woman, living in utter idleness upon
her family, waiting for some man to come along and be beguiled
by his passions and her pretenses into undertaking her support
for life. . . . In her dim, humble way she does her best to live
up to the Henry James ideal of the 'perfect lady'—cultured,
introspective, analytic, loftily contemptuous of all that has to
do with money, *except* spending it."[24] Indeed, even Mrs. Hillis
suggested the establishment of schools where young women
would be taught "to spend" wisely. At any rate, David Graham
Phillips felt that the "New Woman," this "Exotic" whose "life
[is] spent in drifting" from one diversion to another, is an un-
thinkable mate for the American male: ". . . to link the new American woman with the American man is a performance to make
the esthetic to shudder and the practical thunderously to protest.
Only in the very idlest, the very most useless aristocracy could
a proper mate for her be found."[25]

Nevertheless, Phillips recognized the indisputable; namely,

such unfortunate unions—whether prompted by a misguided passion for money or by a reckless sensual drive—do occur. The American wife of the American husband too often becomes what Phillips categorizes as "The Gone-To-Pieces Woman": "... the really dangerous gone-to-pieces woman is she who retains the forms of interest in life—the slovenly gadabout, the purposeless, restless seeker after silly distractions and amusements.... [And] the physically gone-to-pieces woman is she who, through laziness and vanities, will not make an effort."[26]

All manner of fashionable parasites, however, are attracted by superficial glamor of that "foe to ideals," Culture: "The craze for this 'culture' has swept like a pestilence through the land, infecting thousands.... It has a radiating center of infection in almost every college and university in the land.... Its ravages are worse among the women because very few of the men who get 'cultural aspirations' dare indulge them.... 'Culture' calls for days of 'elegant leisure'—and in a world that must work to keep alive, we can have no leisure...."[27] But a leisure class there was, thousands of such moneyed families "whose female members had time to think about how their time should be spent."[28] To members of these fashionable groups and "to many a person along the Fifth Avenues of the nation, whose way of life was being made to appear stupid and vicious, he [Phillips] was another Eugene Debs or Emma Goldman."[29] The title of "Restless Husbands" is therefore a deceptive, even a misleading one, for it offers no analysis or even discussion of the male mystique; it is a heavy attack on what Phillips perceived to be a stagnant, diseased *status quo* that might profit from a series of literary shock treatments.

The enemies of the author were no longer well-fed, Bible-quoting, ruthless plutocrats; at this point he preferred to delineate the "snobbish fake" and to expose "the cult of the antique."[30] The "American girl"—who, even Mrs. Hillis admitted, "has been set up on a pedestal and treated as if she were a superior sort of being"[31]—was, at the hands of an angry novelist, to receive a crude, relentless scrutiny. At times the idealized, sentimental picture of the "eternal feminine" comes across; more often, the prevalent emotions emanating from David Graham Phillips are disenchantment and anger.

II   The Worth of a Woman

During 1907 Phillips wrote a drama, *The Worth of a Woman,* which enjoyed a brief Broadway run starting in February, 1908, and which was notable for the author's presentation of the independent American woman as opposed to the feminine sycophant. Critic Alan Dale in the New York *American* praised the effort heartily, although in a peculiar esthetic patois: "It is a remarkable piece of work, showing keen, logical thought, a daring rush to conclusions, a bold and sportsmanlike grip of an ugly problem. I admire the pluck of this author."[32]

Phillips was undoubtedly aware that "pluck" was the trait an author dealing with sex on the American stage in 1908 needed most; in a preface to *The Worth of a Woman,* he outlined his thoughts on literary morality, summarizing his argument in this way: "Treat the sex question as you would any other question. Don't treat it reverently; don't treat it rakishly. Treat it naturally. Don't insult your intelligence and lower your moral tone by thinking about either the decency or the indecency of matters that are familiar, undeniable, and unchangeable facts of life. Don't look on woman as mere female, but as human being. Remember that she has a mind and a heart as well as a body."[33]

The Hearst syndicate had once described the female type Phillips had in mind: "The bigger the brain, the bigger the heart, not only physically, but sentimentally and morally." The "foolish, ignorant young woman [who] may be pleasing enough to look at" was derided as "a white, pink-eyed rabbit—ornamental."[34] Thus concerned with the transiency of passion, Phillips drew a picture of courageous Diana Merivale whose dedication to "Love and Truth" raises her in the author's eyes to the pinnacle of "womanhood," though "the sewers of conventional hypocrisy" will bubble with jeers for her immorality. It was Lyman Abbott who declared, "From the premiss [*sic*] that marriage is sometimes a species of bondage, reformers have concluded that it should be abolished."[35] Phillips, however, concluded, as had Hearst: "equality" between men and women is "repulsive"; for the "*complete* human being is a man *and* a woman. The *two* make one."[36]

The villainous complication in *The Worth of a Woman* is simply this: Diana Merivale, pregnant, refuses to marry her lover, Julian Burroughs, who, from sense of duty ("reparation"), begs for the opportunity to lift her from this "disgrace." The noble girl feels that Burroughs is enraptured in passion, that he is motivated by his personal sense of honor and by his pity for her degradation, and that he does not love her. Burroughs is sent away ("Begone," thunders Diana's father); but all ends well when he returns, a changed man, the very same evening: "I valued you. But, oh, my God, how I undervalued! Why, not even my own mother ever made me realize that woman, womanhood—is not body, but mind and heart—soul! This afternoon you showed us all what woman can mean. Diana, I was dazed, crushed. I went away hopeless. In the woman I loved I had seen the woman I adored" (105).

Diana, then, triumphed in living by the ideals she had earlier set for herself: "The man I marry . . . must want me—all of me. . . . The man I marry will want a woman, not merely a *female*" (32). Juxtaposed with Diana is her married sister Phyllis, who learned from Aunt Althea that "sex is grossly physical": "The men seeking to possess as cheaply as possible, the women striving to sell as dearly as possible" (20). Phyllis offers the current mythology of courtship ("The safe rule for the woman is to keep the man guessing and grasping. Uncertainty!—charming uncertainty!") and philosophy of marriage (". . . that 'passionate impulse'—it's the way we women get our husbands." [327]). On the other hand Diana was brought up by her widowed father on his extensive farm "in the valley of the Ohio." She was reared "like the Persian youth," Mr. Merivale asserts, "To ride, to shoot, to speak the truth." This "*real* education" has, among other things, transformed Diana into a highly successful business executive ("She's made the whole place over—and it pays like a gold mine—mill, dairies, garden. . . .") capable of assuming a position of responsibility in competitive society.

What Phillips had done, apparently, was to create in Diana Merivale a woman possessing the values attributed by the author to the most admirable and successful men. An antithesis of a parasite, Diana believes in the gospel of work and is revolted by her sister's attitudes ("How cheap you hold men and women," she explodes). Lucius Dagmar, Diana's brother-in-law, recognizes the essential masculinity of the girl: "That's Di," he observes. "Straight as a sapling." His description of her portrays the girl, not as a "weaker vessel," but as a Herculean individualist capable of rising in the Alger world of sink or swim: "I can't think of you except as ranging freely—at a gallop—roads—fences—fields—like a—a Valkyr" (26). Phyllis, too, despite the conventional superficiality of her opinions, recognizes the "secretive and Spartan" (40) traits of her sister.

In reality, then, a world of the triumphant "male animal" is the cosmos holding Phillips' charade of love; the "graceful" Diana, "irradiating open-air freedom," and wearing a "divided riding skirt" is a thoroughly heroic, masculine protest against the artificial, insincere, parasitic American woman of the drawing-room. Phillips should not be taken to task, certainly, for championing the "worth of a woman" as an individual or for assessing high value of a woman as measured in terms of her personal integrity. He must be censured, however, for prizing her solely as an embodiment of manly virtue and for evaluating her by the single yardstick of masculine principle. A rather unusual measurement, indeed, provided the thesis for *The Worth of a Woman*. One must note, however, that in this drama, as in most of his succeeding novels, the Phillips heroine knows when she must capitulate. Several very stubbornly go into seclusion or sail for Europe; but, by the final page, another Brünnhilde fiercely insists, "eyes flashing, her nostrils quivering" with passion: "Crush me! I'll not cry out, unless it is with joy. I love you . . . as they love in the forest where we were at home."[37]

In three of his most important novels—*Old Wives for New* (March, 1908), *The Hungry Heart* (September, 1909), and *The Husband's Story* (September, 1910)—David Graham Phillips took a long, hard look at the institution of marriage in America. Since the more than 72,000 broken marriages in America during 1906 represented twice "the number of divorces in all the remaining Christian world,"[38] the novelist decided to essay a fictional inquiry into this problem and to adjudge its relationship to the New Woman, her scramble for position, leisure, and independence. He thought also to analyze the Male Colossus, his contribution to and his bewilderment at the social delinquency of American womanhood in the new century. Within the

DAVID GRAHAM PHILLIPS

stringent limits of his own substantial prejudices and of his
perfunctory acquaintance with *fin de siècle* sociological and
economic pressures as they related to the "woman question,"
Phillips endeavored to weigh both sides of the marriage contract:
Old Wives for New and *The Husband's Story* are venomous
polemics against a hateful species of an American womanhood
aspiring to sterile leisure; *The Hungry Heart* is a sympathetic
picture of a young adulteress, whose scholar-husband is made,
with a truly *avant-garde* sense of "sportsmanship," to wear with
humility and forgiveness the cuckold's horns.

Percival Pollard, journalist and purveyor of late nineteenth-
century European culture to America, wrote that *Old Wives for
New* atoned for "much slipshod and merely reportorial or
sermonizing writing that Mr. Phillips had done"; that the novel
fortuitously expressed "the doctrine of millions of unconscious
Nietzscheans"; and that Phillips' sketch "of the slatternly wife . . .
proved his emancipation from the ranks of the Great Unsexed."[39]
It was H. L. Mencken, however, who sought to establish for
Phillips, the author "boldly [venturing] upon hazardous psychological laparotomies," a considerable reputation. In "The Leading American Novelist," the sage of Baltimore analyzed nomi-
nations for this title:

> Who is he? Howells? Howells *was*, perhaps, in his time—but
> that was before he began to believe it himself. James? James
> is no more an American than the Sultan of Sulu. Herrick?
> Chambers? McCutcheon? Hopkinson Smith? Dr. Mitchell? Not
> one of those heaven kissing heroes of the $1.08 counter. A lady,
> perhaps? Mrs. Wharton? *See* James, Henry. Mrs. Atherton? Anna
> Katherine Green? Mrs. Eddy? Again no. Get a good grip upon
> the mantel shelf; I am about to name my candidate. He is David
> Graham Phillips. Laugh as much as you like! Laugh until you
> are tired—and then read *The Hungry Heart* and *The Husband's
> Story*.[40]

Literary roustabout Frank Harris went even further: "In my
opinion Phillips is the greatest writer of novels in English,
with much of the power and richness and depth of Balzac
in him." He heaped more effusive encomiums on this prodigy:
"If we compare . . . *Old Wives for New* and *The Husband's Story*
to the best English work of this time we shall see at once

their enormous superiority. George Moore's *Esther Waters* is a pale and feeble pastel in comparison with this vivid, crowded, glowing canvas."[41] Harris concluded with a startling assertion: "One would have to go to the best Russian books, to Tolstoy and Dostoievsky, to meet work of the same quality."[42] And Phillips had "better brains" than Tolstoy! At least one American periodical, however, merely accused Phillips of violating "the instinct for decency" possessed by "millions of Americans."[43]

III Old Wives for New

Both *Old Wives for New* and *The Husband's Story* are detailed chronicles of manners and morals among the plutocrats which chart the road to American divorce courts. Charles Murdock, hero of *Old Wives for New*, had married Sophy Baker, described in the prologue as an embodiment of youthful beauty and shy loveliness—a "nymph." Beginning with the first chapter, Phillips outlines a stark picture of progressive decay on the part of Mrs. Murdock, who, with grown children, servants, and a "luxurious" home, has become a "settled" woman: "she regarded her life as past its climax; and the stage of physical and mental deterioration, indicated in slovenly corpulence, in carelessness of toilet, in stale, monotonous expression of eyes" revealed "dry rot."

Although poor Murdock valiantly tries to beat down his feelings of physical revulsion for his once desirable wife, he hardly succeeds. The love bower is now a nightmare of nausea that Phillips delights in describing: "But every time she twisted or turned there arose from her mop of hair that strong, sour sickening odor to rouse his nerves from oncreeping stupor, to sting them till they quivered. 'Good God!' he muttered, 'surely a little soap and water wouldn't kill her!' " (60). Dr. Schulze blames Sophy's physical collapse and loss of beauty on "over-eating":[44] " 'If you had cared as much for your husband's love as you've cared for pies and cake and candy, you'd not be sitting there, weeping over your sorrows' " (82).

Murdock, meanwhile, under the tutelage of Berkeley, a plutocratic patron of the *demi-monde*, has a brief fling with Viola, whose perfume fires him with reckless passion ("Suddenly he seized her and crushed her in his arms") but whose speech irritates his sense of verbal propriety ("'For God's sake!' he cried, angry as a rudely roused dreamer, 'can't you use decent language?'"). Murdock's real love, though, is Juliet Raeburn, a career girl—a "slender woman, her figure seeming to be vividly alive everywhere within her garments" (305). When he wants freedom from Sophy to marry Juliet, Sophy refuses to divorce him: "Marriage is sacred to me" (162); "O my God, what can I have done that Thou shouldst punish me so?" (164). A train wreck which nearly kills Murdock allows Juliet to disguise as a nurse and to bring him back to health; the accident also brings about the exposure of Blagden, Murdock's conniving secretary who, by catering to Sophy's vanity, wins her heart and hand. The way is soon conveniently clear for Murdock and Juliet, whose voice "like the murmur of a tigress under the caresses of her mate," tells him: "You are angel and devil, both in one. And—I adore you!" (494-95).

IV The Husband's Story

The Husband's Story recounts the same general theme in analyzing the marital disintegration of Edna Wheatlands and Godfrey Loring as they travel together the road from poverty to plutocracy, from the "dreary village" of Passaic, New Jersey, to the wealth-laden drawing-rooms of Paris, London, and Fifth Avenue. In bald, brutal terms, Phillips early in the novel advances the dissident thesis that underlies his clinical tale, related directly by Godfrey Loring, the husband:

> The American woman fancies she is growing away from the American man. The truth is that while she is sitting still, playing with a lapful of the artificial flowers of fake culture, like a poor doodle-wit, the American man is growing away from her. She knows nothing of value; she can do nothing of value. She has nothing to offer the American man but her physical charms, for he has no time or taste for playing with artificial flowers when the world's important work is to be done. So the poor creature grows more isolated, more neglected, less respected, and less sought, except in a physical way. (45)

Loring identifies himself for the benefit of the "Gentle Reader," whom he often addresses directly: "I am a business man, not a smug, shallow-pated failure teaching in an antiquated college.

I abhor the word culture, as I abhor the word gentleman or the word lady..." (11).

The plot of *The Husband's Story* traces the "gaudy gaddings" of Edna throughout the various strata of American society that she tours on her way to the very apex of social achievement: divorce of her husband and the acquisition of a European title. A disillusioned Godfrey watches his wife become infected by "social climbing," "snobbishness," and "toadyism"; he sees his only daughter turned into a title-hunting vixen. As he almost effortlessly cuts corners in the arena of finance to fulfill "the universal American dream of getting up in the world" (82), he becomes a disciple of "shrewd and cynical" Bob Armitage, a business colleague whose attitudes toward the wayward femininity of the nation resemble his own. It is Armitage who explodes: "I have only one strong feeling—and that is my contempt for woman—the American woman" (154). The effete Edna—who squanders all her hours cultivating the "art of leisure" ("art of loafing," says Godfrey), and who, like all American women, was brought up to be a "snob, spender—useless vain parasite"—is at last discarded by her bitter husband. She wastes little time in marrying a worthless nobleman-about-Monte Carlo, the Prince Frascatoni.

Halfway through the novel, however, Loring himself had fallen in love with an American girl, Mary Kirkwood, Armitage's divorced, attractive sister; and her natural, healthy beauty is contrasted with the innate sickliness of "cultured," false Edna. Derived by Phillips from the same lineage as Diana Merivale, the physically robust Mary makes a staggering initial impression on Godfrey Loring as "a woman usefully employed," a girl "actually doing something": "She was in *man's clothes—laboring men's clothes....* She was toiling away with a *gang of men* at clearing the ground where the drains were to center in an artificial lake.... Then she dropped her ax and came forward to meet us. There was certainly *nothing of what is usually regarded as feminine allure* about her. Yet never had I seen a woman more fascinating" (223) [italics mine].

The final page finds Godfrey and Mary, "Alone and free together," sailing past Sandy Hook toward a quiet wedding in Connecticut. Before the yacht has carried the happy lovers off to

the minister's home, Loring, speaking for Phillips, makes facile
summary of the theme he had just dramatized:

> Our whole society is built upon the theory that woman is the
> dependent, the appendage of man. Freedom is impossible for a
> woman, except at a price almost no woman voluntarily pays. To
> have any measure of freedom a woman must bind herself to
> some man, and the bondage has to be cruel indeed not to be
> preferable to the so-called freedom of the unattached female. . . .
> I am glad I was not born a woman. I pity the women of our day,
> bred and cultivated in the tastes of men, yet compelled to be
> dependents, and certain of defeat in a finish contest with
> man. (426)

A husband enables the American woman to enter her elegant
world of "candy and automobiles!—and culture" (159); yet
Godfrey Loring, as he pictures Mary "leading on her gang and
wielding the ax" (223), doubtless regards her as a safe risk
to withstand "the unending flapdoodle" (359) of luxury, fashion,
and gilt.

Charles Murdock of *Old Wives for New* and Godfrey Loring
of *The Husband's Story* are part of a universe whose pulse
throbs by a force not hostile or indifferent, but sympathetic in
a piercing, sentimental manner: "The hardest of the men who
play the game of life with human pawns winces when one of
the pawns shows that it is hurt, sends a human cry of pain into
his very ears; and Murdock, though relentless, was anything
but hard" (454).

The essential Darwinism that seems to underlie a philosophy
of struggle and force is diffused by a vague, chimerical sentiment based on an analogy childlike in its simplicity. Loring
observes the "human animal" and the "powerful thrusts" that
propel it on the journey through life: "The truth is, we are like
flocks of birds in a high wind. Some of us fly more steadily than
others, some are quite beaten down, others seem almost self-
directing; but all, great and small, weak and strong, are controlled by the wind, and those who make the best showing are
those who adapt themselves most skillfully to the will of the
wind" (129).

The responsibility for human agony, therefore, Phillips easily
transfers to a whimsical, capricious force rather than to the

crafty machinations of an Elect motivated by passion and greed. He does not deny the flames of atavism, the "primal impulses" that get "to boiling" (260); yet he creates a blatantly synthetic universe that seems not to exist in reality at all but inhabits solely the polemical values of drawing-room discussion and mercantile-club philosophy. The force that Phillips delineates with clarity in his novels of the business world is conspicuously absent from the tales of marriage and divorce; only a token Darwinist rhetoric remains, but, unfortunately, this literary motif is not made to relate directly to the action.

The major characters in both these tales of men and women in love are, therefore, visible arguments that attempt to dramatize what Phillips' newspaper cohorts would have called "a current human interest." The two male leads are strong, yet genial, plutocrats, who, we are cautiously warned, sin against public morality by shady dealings. Loring scathes the reader with needless, even boorish, abuse: "So it is, gentle reader, though it horrifies your hypocrisy to be told it...." (144); "No doubt you, gentle reader, have fallen asleep over this conversation. I understand perfectly that it is beyond you; for you have no conception of the deep underlying principles of the relations of men and women..." (191). Murdock indirectly assails the reader's intelligence with his alternate moments of blundering self-righteousness—"I let people say what they please. I do what I wish, and presently they tire of railing against me, and say—and think—what I wish them to" (164-65)—or of abject self-effacement: "My life's in ruins—I ruined it. I am an outcast. But I will wander alone" (494). Sophy and Edna, the "gone-to-pieces" women, are counterpointed with Juliet and Mary, graduates of Owen Wister's "Open Air" college of education, "a school that builds character, strengthens courage and develops an American love of liberty."[45] In short, the decadent woman of the parasitic, dissolute metropolis rejects salvation when she turns her back on the strenuous life.

Critics of the two books examined not only Phillips' analyses of marriage in America but also his method and taste. The Los Angeles *Times* noted that the novelist "came near being a second Balzac,"[46] and Frederic Taber Cooper applauded his "craftsmanship that requires a rather masterly touch."[47] William M. Payne, however, reviewing for the *Dial*, dispatched both novels with equal violence. Of *Old Wives for New* he affirmed that "It would be useless to try to find a moral in this incoherent fabrication, which is one of the most revolting books, in both incident and general plan, that we have ever read."[48] Nor did the milk of his critical charity spill over in his treatment of *The Husband's Story*: "Unfortunately, Mr. Phillips has not the equipment of the Juvenal he would like to appear; his generalizations are too sweeping to be impressive, and the incurable vulgarity of his expression excites nothing but disgust."[49] Charlotte Harwood, writing in *Putnam's*, echoed the cry of "vulgarity";[50] the *Outlook* bellowed "disgusting";[51] and the *Nation* chimed in with a similar charge: "Setting out with a theme which is ignoble in most of its external aspects, [Phillips] has not a touch to refine or even to lighten it."[52]

Essentially, the inability of David Graham Phillips to breathe dimension into his characters gives substantial justice to these criticisms. His people, superficially individualized in time and place, seem like replicas of a newspaper tale, so that connection between them and the prototypes of a significant tradition is made impossible. Phillips was hampered in this respect by his contempt for the craft of fiction, by his unbelievable incomprehension of the novelist and his art. Loring, in addition to his numerous fusillades against "culture"—"It is talking in language that means nothing about things that mean less than nothing" (159)—storms against music and literature—those "artistic things": "Oh, those things are all right. . . . But I don't see that it takes any more brains or any better brains to paint a picture or sing a song or write a novel than it does to run a railroad— or to plan one" (44).

V The Hungry Heart

Fiction as an art, to Phillips, coincided with journalism; he failed to perceive that each is motivated by a different esthetic and ethic. He was frenzied as a reporter with a "beat." The newspaper experience that deepened intellectual reservoirs for Norris and Dreiser only made shallower the literary pool from which Phillips drew. His eye for the archetype, the symbol, was dim. He trained his sights on the headline and the rotogravure. The durable was always sacrificed to the timely, and nowhere is this failing better observed than in his treatment of *The Hungry Heart,* ironically, one of his very best efforts and one of the most daring novels of the decade. In it, one should stress, Phillips courageously and admirably, tackled the problem of marital infidelity. His heroine is by no means a "doodle-wit." His hero, however, is not a titan of the business world; he is a reclusive scholar. A modern critic, puzzled at the neglect of this book, appraised the novel as possibly having "done something to bring about a better understanding between men and women [and] a more mature attitude toward wedlock."[53]

The tale follows Richard Vaughan, a research chemist, and his beautiful wife, the former Courtney Benedict, as their honeymoon terminates and they begin their marriage on the Vaughan estate in Wenona, Indiana. Their collision of ideas begins immediately as the affable Vaughan—a pleasing, intelligent gentleman except when "suddenly infuriated by the stealthy fiend of indigestion" (140)—removes himself to the laboratory and informs his astonished bride: "I want you to do your duty as a wife and a mother. . . . I didn't marry a blue-stocking, an unsexed thinking woman. I married a sweet loving wife. . . . I'll not have my home upset" (44). Courtney had entertained hopes of sharing in her husband's life completely; she had even been "brushing up" in her chemistry. First, she is rebuffed with kindly remonstrance: "Wait till you have a baby, and you'll be content to be just a woman" (31); then, by harsh reprimand: "Attend to your house and your baby, like all true women" (45). Courtney, "passive as a doll" (47), is virtually imprisoned in a doll's house.

Richard isolates himself more and more in the laboratory; his neglected wife, "brought up and educated like a man, and then condemned to the old-fashioned life for women" (51), grows sullen and restless. She feels she has "nothing"; her newly born son is "not enough" (51). Her "hungry heart" strains to bring about a complete union with Richard; she realizes they are now touching "only at the surface" (42). Courtney feels the creeping "horror of being a woman" who is "bred to dependence; bred for the market; bred to tease some man into undertaking her support for life" (244-45). She is merely a symbol of her sex at the beck and call of the masculine biological urge and of his status need for a feminine adornment. There is no longer a Courtney Vaughan; she sobs to the uncomprehending, unsympathetic Richard: "This life of ours is a degradation. It's like a stagnant pool—it's death in life" (221). He humors her: "Go on, dear . . . say all you want. You'll feel better for it. . . . Poor child" (221).

In order to expedite his experiments, Vaughan brings an assistant, Basil Gallatin, to live on the estate. Slowly, but inevitably, an infatuation springs up between Gallatin and Courtney: he, passionately in love with her beauty; she, emotionally dependent on his friendship and accessibility. Amid wild and feverish protestations of love, they begin an affair. Courtney, although she first suspects that Gallatin's love for her is purely sensual, begins to idealize her lover with uncritical wonder. Ample opportunity for assignations permits the happy pair to analyze as much as they dare the involvement that has made Basil a "slave" and Courtney a "shameless deceiver." She tells Gallatin: "I'm shocked myself. Somehow I seem to delight in shocking myself—and you. Loving you is—all sorts of pleasures and pains. I want them all!" (178). Gallatin, beaming "like a drunken satyr," cries: "Let's love and be happy. To hell with everything but love" (369).

When Helen March, Vaughan's cousin, comes to stay, Basil states emphatically to his dazed, forlorn mistress that "She's a pure woman. She mustn't be contaminated" (368). Then, continuing to reveal the essential drive behind his passion, he confesses to the horrified Courtney that "It's because I love you that I go crazy at the thought that I'm sharing you" (369). At this statement, the days of Courtney's self-deception are over; she recalls Gallatin's "sensual, maudlin face" and knows "he did not love"; she realizes her very own responsibility in his emotional "fraud" (372).

Thus, Vaughan at last discovers his wife's deceit; and he reveals himself as forgiving and lofty-minded to an uncharacteristic degree: ". . . I'm grateful to—to whatever it was—fate or chance or what you please—for my awakening. But for it, what'd have become of me?" (430). Courtney realizes the true motivation for her "hungry heart": "I was swept away by my craving for love—for what Richard in our brief honeymoon had taught me to need" (465). A dishonest, dudish Basil, formerly so virtuous in her distorted vision, now appears a fading second to her husband: "Her glance darted from Richard leaning calmly against the table and, in blouse and cap, looking like a handsome workingman, to Basil in his fashionable English tweeds, standing shamefaced and irresolute near the door..." (472). The "paralyzed Gallatin, denounced by Courtney as a "shabby coward" is dismissed from her life; but Richard must be exposed to a merciless verbal flaying—"... I have kissed him and caressed him and trembled with passion for him as I never did for you...." (473)—before an ultimate reconciliation. It is Vaughan who finally begs forgiveness as Courtney sobs, "I've found it!"

Phillips' chronic penchant for the neat wrap-up led to a harassed, chaotic conclusion with surface emotion pushed to limits of human hysteria—a chemical vial with ingredients to kill is even used to intensify the melodrama. Yet this intellectual confusion reflected the author's nervous treatment of a dilemma whose resolution Phillips felt would be unpopular. With commendable courage he assailed the Nietzschean woman (breeder of children) and ornamental wife; he scathed the superior husband zealously possessive of his supposed intellectual advantage and neglectful of his wife's aspirations for individuality. Then, an adulterous wife was forgiven by a noble husband who begs *her* pardon. Such an eventuality ran counter to demands of propriety and convention. Phillips, further, gave a detailed presentation of the primitive passion overwhelming Basil and Courtney: "He went round behind her, drew out the hairpins one by one, fumbling softly, lingeringly for them, keeping them carefully. Her hair loosened, uncoiled, fell about her in a shimmering veil. 'Oh, my love!' he cried.... And he took the soft, perfumed veil in his hands, kissed it again and again, buried his face in it, wrapped her head and his together in it" (177).

The price of such courage in 1909, however, was a reaction from some quarters both denunciatory and withering. William M. Payne of the *Dial* was again lying in critical ambush for *The Hungry Heart;* but his evaluation of this daring novel failed to match the vituperation emanating from his colleagues on the other journals. Nevertheless, Payne's observations cannot be considered favorable in any sense: "Unfortunately, Mr. Phillips, who can write verbosely and expound a thesis with a good deal of vehemence, cannot shape consistent character and cannot avoid the pitfalls of vulgarity and sensationalism. He keeps our sympathies constantly shifting."[54] The *Literary Digest* questioned Phillips' concept of morality: "It is a book one would hardly care to read aloud in the family circle. The novel is not convincing and the cynical tendency it exhibits in railing at human nature and existing conditions is not uplifting."[55]

While the *Nation* affirmed that *The Hungry Heart* "is a vigorous tract,"[56] the New York *Times* in unfavorably reviewing the novel stressed the opinion that the failure of the book corresponds to the failure of Phillips' entire literary execution: "It is not the theme which is in itself repellent; it is the lack of artistic balance, the insistence on details which have no value, moral or artistic, to the working out of the story, and that fixed idea which is becoming an unpleasantly prominent feature in Mr. Phillips's work which render the book unattractive. He is mistaken in his method of presenting his ideas, which are often well worth while."[57]

Thus what Phillips had regarded as a bold thrust into the conventional fabric of the social mores served as a basis in this eminently respectable newspaper for his appraisal as a writer who expounds worthy ideas but who is an incompetent technician. Yet, after one praises the courage (recklessness?) behind *The Hungry Heart*, he must even question the charitable *Times* and its testimony to the value of Phillips' ideas. Abounding in his usual seriousness, Phillips, a health faddist, stated with conviction that "indigestion" is "the chief cause of humanity's faults of temperament, from morbidness to acute mania" (140). Such an outrage to intelligence is buttressed conclusively by the recurrence of the author's *sententiae* and their revelation of life's wisdom: "A man always takes to the best-looking woman" (336); "Like so many women, she doesn't realize that corset is three-fourths of the battle for figure" (274); "Life must be lived, and with human beings" (373). More than shallowness, an intellectual vacuum is apparent.

Nor could Phillips transcend the Romantic idiom of the fiction of his day he railed against as perpetrated by "stupid, unthinking writers, pandering to the stupid unthinking public!"[58] H. L. Mencken, in praising Phillips, had attacked contemporary American fictionists by claiming that "the purpose of novel writing, as that crime is practiced in the United States, is not to interpret life, but to varnish, veil and perfume life . . . with music by Victor Herbert."[59] One can with justice defend Phillips in his use of controversial social situations revolving about infidelity and divorce; yet his concept of Realism and his ear for the vernacular of the Romancer are inextricably mired in his times. A Grosset & Dunlap advertisement for a popular novel, Porter Emerson Browne's *A Fool There Was*, can reveal the small arc of truth and tiny province of verisimilitude inhabited by many bestselling contemporary authors and, despite his protests, by David Graham Phillips: "A relentless portrayal of the career of a man who comes under the influence of a beautiful but evil woman; how she lures him on and on, how he struggles, falls and rises, only to fall again into her net, makes a story of *unflinching realism*" [italics mine].[60]

Phillips went about the task of constructing pasteboards of humanity in truthful, authentic postures; but in *The Hungry Heart* he was betrayed by his inability to avoid the extravagance of declamation—"You streamer of flame that's burning up my soul" (346)—or of exaggerated prattle: "'What a cur I am!' he exclaimed, put to shame by her sigh and her forlorn expression" (359). When Phillips writes that "His menacing glance did not daunt her," (395) he cannot be accused of the cliché but indicted for following the paths exploited with great market success by his coterie of fellow Romancers whose company he liked to think he diligently avoided. Then too, some of the secret meetings between Basil and Courtney are downright funny because of the author's "Realism":

"Dawn! I must fly. Where *are* my slippers!" (179)

.   .   .   .

"Courtney, we've been—and are—in the clutch of a force that's stronger than we." (183)

.   .   .   .

"Be careful," she whispered. "The floor was polished only yesterday." (365)

Here Phillips pays the literary penalty of the honest explorer into the daring, gloomy byways of the social contract, a writer whose flaming sincerity far exceeds his competence. The sex theme of *The Hungry Heart* grew simply too big for Phillips to control. He lacked the esthetic equipment and the moral insight for so ambitious a probing into the psychology of his characters.

There were lesser dimensions to the "woman problem," however, that held fascination for Phillips; questions that might beguile the creator of Hollywood scenarios danced through his mind as likely material for books: a romance between a Socialist firebrand and a daughter of the plutocracy? the love of a gentleman of fashion for an emancipated, radical female? the courtship and marriage of a society dame and a society-hating senator from the West? All these possibilities eventually became realities for David Graham Phillips, as his feverish pen flashed like a productive charm. He was to raise the curtain on his version of the "class struggle"; but it would be a battle with only faint Marxist overtones. From the people of the abyss and their common lot, to the hand-made gentleman and his slavery to success, Phillips, a one-man factory of fiction, spun tales of love and ambition in the small, ordered universe he had comfortably created as his own.

CHAPTER 7

The Lady of the Decoration

NOW THAT David Graham Phillips had oriented his literary energy toward examining various phases in the adjustment of the New Woman in American society during its "strenuous age," he began to experiment with a variety of moral confrontations involving different feminine temperaments suddenly faced by social exigencies and political expediencies of the time. To all appearances, his rather free-and-easy treatment of this popular theme appealed to readers of *Cosmopolitan* and the *Saturday Evening Post;* for, while aspiring to be regarded as a social theorist, Phillips became securely linked to the chain of voluble Romancers.

In three novels—*The Fashionable Adventures of Joshua Craig* (1909), *The Conflict* (1911), and *George Helm* (1912)—he utilized his one-time favorite diversion of politics and love; more explicitly, the love of a society woman for a politician who springs from the "lower class." These novels, none of which received distinguished reviews in the critical organs, carried Phillips back in time to the pre-"Treason" days when his characters, both male and female, alternately stalked the Stock Exchange and the Treasury Department. In this new phase he surveyed the conditions of courtship and marriage between legislators and their women as they traveled from the rustic society of grange and county seat to the awesome fountainhead of diplomatic wisdom in Washington. Previously, Phillips had been primarily interested in political corruption and social whirligigs; now he was concerned mostly with love and the woman's reaction to it.

I The Fashionable Adventures of Joshua Craig

The Fashionable Adventures of Joshua Craig is set in the
malevolent wilds of Washington, D.C.; and there a turbulent
senator from the hinterlands of the West falls recklessly in love
with a society lady who has secretly contrived to marry him.
While the background of this slight tale had been adequately
sketched by the author several years before in *The Social
Secretary*, Elbert Hubbard noted in his "little magazine" that the
protocol of life in the shadow of "receptions, fetes, soirees, din-
ners and teas" inflicted upon public servants their accompanying
social sycophants:

> Politically, we live in the Age of Snobbery. That is to say, the
> social period of imitation and uncertainty. Socially the city of
> Washington is imitating the Old World nobility and out-
> Heroding Herod. Washington Society is clutching for Respect-
> ability thru Strenuous, Conspicuous Waste of time and material.
> And that it is succeeding in its complete devotion to futility, none
> can deny.[1]

Josh Craig, however, is a different breed of man; he tells his
friend, the dandy Arkwright: " 'But, damn it, Grant, I'm not
civilized. I'm a wild man, and I'm going to stay wild. I belong
to the common people, and it's my game—and my preference,
too—to stick to them. . . . I know that to play the game here in
Washington I've got to do something in society. But . . . I'm
still going to be myself. I'll make 'em accept me as I am' " (6-7).
Yet the candid Josh possesses some drives that go beyond the
ambitions of even the most grasping, success-frenzied Horatio
Alger hero. The senator confides to Arkwright the corrupt base
of his ravening aspirations: " 'But I don't want money, I want
power—to make all these snobs with their wealth, these mil-
lionaires, these women with fine skins and beautiful bodies, bow
down before me—that's what I want! . . . and I'll get what I
want—the people and I' " (34).

Miss Margaret Severance is one of the "fashionable noddle-
heads" (264) in Washington society. A twenty-eight-year-old
"spinster," she plans to marry Craig and to rechannel his
abundance of frontier energy into proper social pursuits. Their

mutual passion is quickly discovered: "despite her protests and struggles, she was again in those savage arms of his . . . burning and trembling under his caresses" (144). They marry, and Josh takes the subdued and shocked Margaret away from the temptations of Washington to his home town of Wayne, Minnesota, where he will be drafted to run for governor. Craig carries his tearful wife from "unearned luxury" and a "purposeless life" among the fashionable set. Throughout the book, rugged Josh is contrasted with weak, gentlemanly Arkwright, whose love for Margaret, too long unexpressed, is never to be fulfilled. Craig tells the discouraged suitor, "Believe me, Grant, you don't understand women. They don't like you delicate fellows. They like a man—like me—a pawer of the ground—a snorter—a warhorse that cries ha-ha among the trumpets" (85). And, indeed, if one might regard Miss Severance as a valid case study, the senator from Minnesota is correct; for what began on her part as a flirtatious caprice eventually drove the calculating Margaret into paroxysms of rapture: "You fill me with a kind of—of—horror. You draw me into your grasp in spite of myself—like a whirlpool and rouse all my instinct to try and save myself." The genial Josh laughs complacently and theorizes, "That is love" (267). Her "society" is a "debaucher of manhood" (79); Craig is of "the people."

Thus Phillips reduced the Class Struggle to a simple contest of drawing-room versus log cabin. The stakes, a congenial marriage:

[Margaret] ". . . the social side of life can be very useful in
        furthering a man."
[Joshua] "In furthering a lick-spittle—yes. But not a *man!*" (328)

His marriage to Margaret will not bring Senator Craig "instant status"; it will bring moral ruination unless the salubrious effect of the great plains can act as spiritual antidote. The poison of tinsel and frivolity must be purged. The gospel of work and do, so dear to Phillips, is emblemized in Craig's hard and rough ambition. Its antithesis is stated by Margaret's sister: "Everybody that's nice ought to have money . . . then the world would be beautiful, full of love and romance, with everybody clean and well-dressed and never in a hurry" (107). As the book ends, a trainman is calling to Mrs. Margaret Severance Craig, "Hurry up, lady, or you'll get left!" (365). She has gone to Minnesota and the log-cabin for a fresh start toward the White House!

II The Conflict

David Graham Phillips took a closer look at his libidinous version of the Class Struggle in *The Conflict;* in it there actually is a direct clash between the hosts of Socialism and the legions of Democracy. Remsen City, Indiana, a mill and railroad town, is a center of radical activity; for, emanating from its sooty environs and "gentle hills" is the *New Day,* a workingman's newspaper, published by Victor Dorn, whom Phillips apparently modeled after Eugene V. Debs.[2] Falling precipitantly in love with Dorn is Jane Hastings, daughter of a local plutocrat who is a bitter enemy of Socialism. The infatuation of Dorn and the socialite, which transcends party lines, is mutual ("If I'm in your power, you're in my power too" [264]); but the proletarian champion realizes that he can never marry perverse, power-hungry Jane. He rejects the defiant beauty with this noble explanation: "I would become a member of your class, but would pose as a representative of the class I had personally abandoned" (279). Phillips manages to keep the pairings separate but equal, as he finally unites Dorn with his left-wing, half-Jewish, editorial assistant, the intellectual Selma Gordon; and Jane finds her love in an ambitious doctor who entertains some radical "ideas." This theme of class separation is examined further in Selma Gordon's romance with Davy Hull, a fashionable politician. Hull adores Selma; but, when he declares his love, she turns on him fiercely: "You miserable fraud! You bellwether for the plutocracy. . . . I despise you" (334).

In a brief epilogue to the novel Phillips notes that the Workingman's League now controls Remsen City: Victor Dorn and his principles have at length triumphed. *The Conflict,* then, is Phillips' warmest courting of Socialism since *The Second Generation,* when reviewers presented him as a hopeless visionary with anti-democratic sentiments. Phillips, certainly, was no Socialist in 1907, nor was he in 1911. Yet, he was able to amalgamate elements of both the political radical and the rugged advocate of sterling Americanism into his ethic. In *The Conflict*

Doctor Charlton flays millionaire Martin Hastings when Jane's
father, ill-advisedly, uses the term "conservative":

> It gags me to hear it. *You're* not a conservative. If you had
> been you'd still be a farm hand. You've been a radical all your
> life—changing things round and round, always according to
> your idea of what was to your advantage. The only difference
> between radicals like you robber financiers and radicals like
> Victor and me is that our ideas of what's to our advantage
> differ. . . . You want the world changed—laws upset, liberty de-
> stroyed, wages lowered . . . so that you can get all the money.
> We want the world changed so that we can be healthy and com-
> fortable and happy. . . . (291)

Industrialist Hastings, then, is really a radical! And Dr.
Charlton completes his ingenious circle by moving the politics
of Victor Dorn more toward the center: "Leaders like Victor
Dorn . . . seem new and radical today. By tomorrow they'll be
the commonplace thing, found everywhere . . ." (292). Indeed,
while the riot in Market Square has faint overtones of the Haymarket Riot and while Phillips has Selma lecture Jane on Marx
and Christ ("Both were Jews, [and] labor agitators" [62]), one
feels the romance more than the polemic; there is no doctrinal
clash between two political ideologies. Rather, there is a feeble
attempt at a reconciliation of radicalism and conservatism as
springing from one singular source: the sensible quest for power.
Even Hastings regards Davy Hull with a scorn not unlike Selma
Gordon's: "Them political fellows are a lot of blackmailers," he
asserts (295). For Victor Dorn, Hastings has more than a
modicum of understanding and sympathy: "I never have blamed
him—not really. . . . A practical man—a man that's been through
things—he understands how these things are. . . . Yes, I reckon
Victor's doing the best he can—getting up by the only ladder
he's got a chance at" (102).

And even Dorn himself contributes to this festival of understanding and respect by evincing a sound appreciation of the
financier in American society: "It's very interesting—how much
there is in a minute and in a dollar if you're intelligent about
them" (106). Phillips eventually blames environment as the
flywheel of motive in the behavior of his people: "As I told
you before . . . it's conditions that make the human animal what-

ever it is. It's in the harness of conditions—the treadmill of conditions—the straight jacket of conditions. Change the conditions
and you change the animal" (295). In *The Conflict,* too, Phillips
decided not to present a challenge in this neat dramatization
of the conflicts in society. His characters are rigid. He refused
to expose proletarians Dorn and Selma to the decadent luxury
of the plutocracy; he denied patrician Jane Hastings the
experience of working in a sweatshop and living in a slum.

III George Helm

George Helm, serialized in *Hearst's Magazine* (April-Septem-
ber, 1912), continued to explore the "class warfare" in terms of
love, marriage, and caste. While the themes of corruption,
graft, and power, which serve as background for the novel,
indicate that Phillips probably composed *George Helm* during
the pre-"Treason" period[3] when his major interests lay in
dissecting the political animal, his central thesis remained very
close to that of *The Conflict.* Here is pictured the romance of
Helm, a dirt-poor, small-town lawyer who is lured into politics
by dreams of doing honest good and who falls in love with
Eleanor Clearwater, the daughter of a lumber king. Helm
offers Eleanor no delusions about what their marriage will be
like: "You understand you're leaving your class and coming to
mine—and that the war between these two classes is going to
be bitter and more bitter..." (247).

Clearwater excoriates Helm, intent on good government, as a
dangerous demagogue opposed to the ideals sacred to "the
republic of the fathers": "To get office, to lift yourself, you are
willing to rouse the ignorant and the idle to hate and to assault
the men whom God has raised up to develop and to guard this
country!...Anarchy and socialism aren't political opinions....
They're criminal, sir, criminal" (219-20). Like Josh Craig, Helm
is vaguely of the people. He is a rugged individualist ("I don't
hope—I work" [39]) who redeems the hour as successfully as
plutocrat Clearwater. He is eminently (and Phillips stresses this
term throughout the novel) "sensible," not at all radical: "His
crusading spirit was not either academic or fanatic. It was the
sensible indignation of the man who discovers that a certain
evil has gone far enough and must be put down" (124).

Helm's instinct "for the feeling of the people" eventually sweeps him into the governor's mansion where he must crush his father-in-law's corporate "doggeries" in timber to fulfill campaign promises of "honest administration." In a scene of extravagant melodrama, Clearwater, the trapped villain, feels he has been betrayed as a sacrifice to the political prosperity of his son-in-law: "I shall disinherit you, I shall curse you. I shall curse you, I shall curse you" (290). Eleanor and George, bathed in tears of love, return to the mansion where Helm will begin to plan an "independent movement" (301) free from the corruption in both major parties.

Most important as theme of *George Helm* is the powerful stream of sentiment directed against "the people" and their gullible susceptibility to panacea promoters. In the constant "struggle between warring appetites, between competing selfishnesses" (277), is generated a need, Phillips feels, for the occasional appearance of a Saviour: "The Jews of ancient days are not the only people who have dreamed of a Messiah. The Messiah-dream, the Messiah-longing has been the dream and the longing of the whole human race, toiling away in obscurity, oppressed, exploited, fooled, despised. Hence, news of leaders springing up spreads fast and far among the people" (123). The people are "waiting always for the leaders" (124) to remove the reasons for their discontent. To a political ward heeler in the book, "the people are mutts...born to be trimmed" (69). For Clearwater, the timber king, the "masses" are characterized by their "ass-like patience, their worm-like meekness" (211). Even George Helm himself takes a dim view of the electorate that voted him into office: "If there were a real 'people'—intelligent, persistent, not easily fooled, no longer conquerable and easy to rob and oppress through their ignorance and their prejudices—if there were 'the people,' refusing to be ruled except by and for themselves, what a heaven of a world it would become!" (302-3). There is enough of the opportunist in Helm, however, to realize that, whether the "people" deserve representative government or despotic plunder, each ballot counts; and he informs Harvey Sayler, who appears in the novel to urge upon Helm the mantle of kingmaker, that the "sweeping current" of popular support is a reality worth courting. George, visions of playing the savior dancing before him, chooses to swim with it.

Craig, Dorn, and Helm are in slightly modified degrees and in a variety of expressions portraits of the identical messiah come to raise up "the people." Each man is imbued with a substantial sense of mission and authoritarianism; each is relentless. The three are crude in character, conduct, and dress. None knows how to navigate with ease among the socially sophisticated; in false opposition to each, manners are equated with weakness and lack of direction. Simultaneously, they are true believers and wooden participants in the human conflict surrounding them; but, for each of these major protagonists, Phillips beclouds the issues with his characteristic passion theme. These politically oriented heroes are sexually inflamed by "Superior Class" women; more than coincidentally, too, the involved women are stirred by the brutal virility of the messianic trio. In the novels, however, Phillips never actually came to grips with the appearance of the messiah and his direct relationship to the anxious masses: the author's three Nietzschean dynamos drift off at length to embark upon fresh, ambiguous campaigns for the political redemption of the reprobate.

The *Dial* (nemesis Payne again) dismissed *The Fashionable Adventures of Joshua Craig* for its "unredeemed vulgarity";[4] the *Times* flayed the "immature grasp of life" portrayed in *The Conflict*[5] and the "tiresome and wooden" characters in *George Helm*.[6] At the base of these critical ambuscades, however, is a general proposition that Phillips had created characters in a syndrome of type-psychology that he imperfectly understood. The superficiality of their motives defied analysis and fell short of challenging theorists of a new century more than mildly curious about exploring the relationships of science and spirit, of mind and time. Phillips endowed his three would-be paradise planters with a facile Nietzschean facade; animal passion was the only response that a breeder of children could hope to excite in these "supermen" of deific proportions. Phillips, indeed, remained in the past with his journalese simplicities to reflect the ailment of his era. Devastating to him was the newspaper appraisal that observed "[Phillips'] crudeness of the conceptions and the unreality of the personages puts a heavy drag upon . . . the reader at all thoughtful [or] perspicacious."[7]

IV White Magic

In June, 1909, Phillips wrote to George Horace Lorimer concerning his latest tale of courtship and marriage: "Unless you think badly of it make the title of that story *White Magic*—That's a nice poetical name for love that heats and overheats—makes a snobbish girl romantic and an ambitious artist a lover.... However, you may not like it—If so, I'll try again...."[8] The title stood, and the *Saturday Evening Post* began in November to serialize a novel that must be recognized as a rewrite of *Her Serene Highness,* the Graustarkian atrocity Phillips had perpetrated some seven years earlier. While the scene is geographically moved, the action and artifice remain constant: the art collector of the earlier novel now becomes an artist; the princess in her mythical kingdom becomes a daughter of the plutocracy in her father's ostentatious palace in the isolated wilderness of northern New Jersey; the villainous prince and the heavy-hearted father have counterparts of equal importance in *White Magic,* which, as the *Nation* charitably noted, circulates among "the airy draperies of social comedy."[9]

Artist Roger Wade spends most of the novel rejecting Beatrice Richmond, spoiled and willful, who loves the elusive painter ("All I know is, I *must* have *him.*" [121]). Her father objects and means to carry out monstrous threats against his daughter's lover: "I'll beggar that artist and drive him out in disgrace.... In two days I can have him made penniless" (208). Beatrice is "imprisoned" within the confines of the estate and is kept under constant surveillance by "watchmen" and "patrolmen" lest she slip away to a rendezvous with Wade. She luckily manages to elude burglar alarms, superintendents, and a variety of family retainers; thus escaping, she informs the artist of her plight. Beatrice eventually runs away from home; her father at last consents to her marrying the aloof painter; and Phillips' society farce terminates in a delirium of love ("How well we understand each other! How congenial we are!" [392]).

A brief but intense spasm of domestic rebellion is portrayed in Beatrice's leaving the "swarm of idlers" who constitute her environment to flee to New York where she intends "to be free" (203). An unconventional woman, Beatrice makes all of the

amatory advances; and, though a sheltered patrician educated
to female reticence, she quickly confesses to the frantic biological
hunger aroused in her by Wade: "Suddenly she flung her arms
round his neck, kissed him passionately, her embrace tight..."
(142-3). Away from home, the urge for complete emancipation
sweeps over Beatrice; she will enter the business world, start a
dressmaking shop: "I want everybody to know," she tells her
alarmed father, "because I intend to make loads and loads of
money. You've no idea of the profits in fashionable dressmaking.
Eighty—a hundred—a hundred and fifty per cent!" (325). Here
is no idler. Motivated by passion and ambition, the defiant Miss
Richmond will succeed in the masculine world as formidably as
any of Phillips' male heroes.

V   The Grain of Dust

In February, 1911, when Lorimer began to serialize *The Grain
of Dust,* readers of the *Post* were introduced to twenty-one-year-
old Dorothea Hallowell, Phillips' only clock-punching, working-
girl heroine. Dorothea enchants her employer, attorney Frederick
Norman, to such precipitous desire that he forsakes career and
fashionable fiancée to pursue his reluctant, bewitching clerk-
typist. Fred Norman has been methodical and ruthless in his
climb to the top of the legal profession; like a machine, he had
thundered and rolled over the human obstacles that had crowded
the road before him. Now, metaphorically, "A grain of dust,
dropped into [his] watch movement in just the right place..."
(345) effectively brought his entire career to ruin. Lightheaded
with passion, he wanders in drunken stupor among his bewildered associates and comes to life only in the presence of
the innocently seductive Dorothea, whom he courts wildly: "'I
am mad about you—mad. You *must* understand. I can think only
of you. I am insane with jealousy of you. I want you—I must
have you.'... He rained kisses upon her pale face.... 'I will
teach you to love me,' he cried, drunk now with the wine of
her lips, with the perfume of her exquisite youth. 'I will make
you happy. We shall be mad with happiness'" (135). As
frequently as he can maneuver the situation, Norman seizes
Dorothea and "rains kisses" over the alternately dazed, pained,
and astonished face of this "fatal woman."

At last the persistently unwilling Dorothea, impressed by Norman's philanthropic subsidy of her father's chemical laboratory and weakened by his steady assault on her virtue, capitulates: "I am willing to marry you. . . . I am so tired of struggling . . ." (319). The invigorated lawyer soon scrambles back to the top; and the marriage, which teeters unsteadily when his rabid appetite cools, at last reaches a happy, mature plateau with children and pleasant domesticity. Phillips' theme, then, revolves about passion, an uncontrollable physical phenomenon, and its psychic force; he sincerely believed that among contemporary American novelists only he portrayed sex as not evoking "paranoiac egotism, but a generous and beautiful kind of unselfishness" (315).

In *The Grain of Dust*, Phillips also presented a virulent tirade against the use of psychology in literature by his fellow writers. His words rang with an incensed anger that perhaps compensated for the dark folklore he energetically presented as fact:

> Soon it will be no longer possible for the historian and the novelist, the dramatist, the poet, the painter or sculptor to present in all seriousness as instances of sane human conduct, the aberrations resulting from various forms of disease ranging from indigestion in its mild, temper-breeding forms to acute homicidal or suicidal mania. In that day of greater enlightenment a large body of now much esteemed art will become ridiculous. Practically all the literature of strenuous passion will go by the board or will be relegated to the medical library where it belongs; and it, and the annals of violence . . . will be cited as documentary proof of . . . low economic and hygienic conditions. . . . For certain it is that the human animal when healthy and well fed is invariably peaceable and kindly and tolerant—up to the limits of selfishness, and even encroaching upon those limits. Of writing rubbish about love and passion there is no end—and will be no end until the venerable traditional nonsense about those interesting emotions shares the fate that should overtake all the cobwebs of ignorance clogging the windows and walls of the human mind. (314-15)

Phillips derides the "fiddle-faddle concerning passion" as a destructive emotion when, paradoxically, *The Grain of Dust* illustrates the view he is attacking. Norman's furious love never fails to terrify Dorothea; his "delirium of pride and possession" frightens her into running away from him during the first week of their marriage. She soon must adjust to being a quiet fixture in the circuit of his dynamic, even brutal, personality. The individualism of Dorothea is broken as she becomes a domestic ornament; her unique and mysterious loveliness is destroyed as a mere myth deriving from Norman's procreant urge. Her singular quality of mind is obliterated; her husband will "educate [this] not too difficult woman to be his wife" (397). It is indeed perplexing to see how Phillips, whose insight into human character and motivation seldom went beyond the digestive tract, could with ease score the clinical followers of Zola, or even the tawdry disciples of a McCutcheon or a Ouida. His own visceral criticism echoes with the thin resonance of peripheral analysis and his unfortunate bias toward oversimplification. Passion, which Poe had excluded from his poetics as a degrading emotion, was haphazardly employed by Phillips as an artless vehicle for generating the singular tension of his novel. His sad excursion into the misfortunes of psychology in the hands of the creative artist only intensifies the amateurish tone and unwholesome naïveté of his slender "philosophical system." Certainly, Phillips' open contempt for scholarship never led him to a study of the principles he so wisely doubted.

Yet Phillips honestly felt that he was in a rising vanguard of authors who would reveal in due time the fallacies clinging to the myth of women in American civilization. A clear and vibrant epitome of the new romancers of early twentieth-century American letters, he castigated in *The Grain of Dust* that ignorance taught "about the human heart" by preachers, novelists, and poets: "Literature and the drama, representing life as it is dreamed by humanity, life as it perhaps may be some day, create an impression which defies the plain daily and hourly mockings of experience" (366). In details of action, however, Phillips' triumphant heroes and heroines surmounted their difficulties in the familiar style of unbelievable derring-do. His portrait of the beautiful Dorothea looking "positively homely" over breakfast coffee was regarded by Phillips as courageous honesty offering a true picture of life as it is. But his heroines seldom looked homely for long.

VI The Price She Paid

Serialized in *Cosmopolitan* (October, 1911–July, 1912), *The Price She Paid*, while it contains the same superficial psychology characteristic of his other love tales, anticipates several of the social concerns that were to occupy the author's attention in *Susan Lenox*. The novel also presents one of his most vivid creations—megalomaniacal General Siddall, a martinet in elevator heels. The major character is Mildred Gower, formerly a daughter of fashionable society who now, because of the death of her wealthy uninsured father and the remarriage of her mother to a man of little means, must make her own way in the world though she is totally unfit for earning a living. Phillips closes the first chapter on this dilemma with a symbol reminiscent of the literary methods of Frank Norris:

> When she was a child she leaned from the nursery window one day and saw a stable-boy drowning a rat that was in a big, oval, wire cage with a wooden botton. The boy pressed the cage slowly down in the vat of water. The rat, in the very top of the cage, watched the floor sink, watched the water rise. And as it watched it uttered a strange, shrill, feeble sound which she could still remember distinctly and terribly. It seemed to her now that if she were to utter any sound at all, it would be that one. (40-41)

Mildred tries to escape the approaching days of poverty by marrying a robber baron, Siddall, a psychotic little general whose specialty is marrying girls of limited financial means and imprisoning them in his own version of the "gilded cage." He gives them no money but lavishes luxuries upon them—so long as his lascivious appetites are satiated; his icy, mechanical manner Phillips coordinated well with the ogrish, rodent-like appearance he makes to disillusioned Mildred. "My dear," he benignly says by way of proposal, "I find that I am ready to go the limit—if you are" (84). This "mysterious and terrible" personality, this "grotesque little figure" enjoys buying clothes for his wife and "inspecting the finery for himself"; he "loves" adorning his "property" in the "most delicate of hand-made underwear," and established charge accounts for Mildred in the very best Parisian shops. For this generosity he demands uncompromising, docile obedience, and complete servility ("Don't keep me waiting. It's chilly. ..." [192]).

The very antidote to passion, Siddall inspires frigidity in Mildred. She leaves his bed, and discovers that she is a literal prisoner in his home and in Paris. His detectives shadow her every move. Like the master in control of numberless robots, Siddall undertakes various persecutive campaigns to bring Mildred to her knees. Fortunately, she succeeds in returning for cash an expensive purse the general had bought her; and the bewildered, terrified woman managed the exchange an instant before Siddall swooped down upon this shop to thwart his wife's attempt to raise money. Mildred sails to America, but for the next several months General Siddall in his "monotonous, almost lifeless" and methodical manner pursues and watches, chases and observes, playing a vast game of torture. Occasionally he confronts and warns his prey: "I never let anyone break a bargain with me without making them regret it" (152). His face, a mask "devoid of expression," nevertheless conveys to harassed Mildred "a sense of malignance unutterable eyeing her from behind a screen."

Phillips manages with real skill to convey the sense of un-reality surrounding Siddall, as well as the horror of his cold, vindictive passion for vengeance: "It was the lean, little face with the funny toupee and needle-like mustache and imperial, but behind it lay a personality like the dull, cold, yellow eyes of the devilfish ambushed in the hazy mass of dun-colored formlessness of collapsed body and tentacles" (153). Phillips, however, failed to realize the possibilities in terms of symbol and suspense represented by General Siddall; nor was he capable of exploring the abnormal psychology implicit in the general's patterns of behavior, for soon the little man, revealed as a bigamist who can no longer tyrannize Mildred, is dropped. The novel deteriorates quickly: Mildred goes to New York, lives for a brief time in a "bird cage," but moves out when she discovers the nature of her surroundings. She studies voice and begins to sing in musical revues on Broadway. The final problem before her involves a choice between marriage and a career. The career wins, and Mildred rushes "away to fresh triumphs" (379) on the stage. She "had leaped from obscurity into fame" (376), and love will be an entertainment "for a holiday" (376). Mildred Gower's success, Phillips asserts, points the accusing finger at the cowardly who quickly surrender to the ease of bird cages and at the slothful who are "too lazy to work" (326).

Despite its counterfeit preachments toward the morality of American women, *The Price She Paid* attracted at least faint praise from one female critic: Margaret Sherwood in the *Atlantic* called it "better" than any other Phillips novel she had read.[10] Compared to other estimates, however, this view was extravagant; for the *Nation* labeled the novel "crudity without force"[11] and the *Independent* thoroughly annihilated Mildred Gower's decay and regeneration: "A more unpleasant book of repulsive people we have seldom read. There is the same shallow psychology, the same lack of discrimination, the same bad taste, which characterizes the author's most popular work."[12] Actually, the "unpleasant" and uncomfortable scenes are the best in the novel: those of the leering general with the overtones of psychopathic degeneracy about him. Mildred's sudden rise to fortune, her noble avoidance of marriage, and the ultimate Romantic perfume for the fictional package suffocate some of Phillips' strongest writing.

VII *Degarmo's Wife*

Two years after Phillips' death, D. Appleton and Company brought out *Degarmo's Wife*, a collection of three stories of love and marriage that had appeared earlier in popular magazines[13] —the title story, "Enid," and "White Roses and Red." "Degarmo's Wife" is a retelling of his early story "The First-Born": like the young husband pictured in the tale of 1891, Joe Degarmo stares out of the window and silently laments the apparent passing of his wife's love for him: "She is no longer a wife. She is a mother!" he despairs. Phillips had stopped the tale there in its first version for *Harper's Weekly*. Now, however, he has Norma hire a baby sitter for the child, begin to "fight bust and hips," and "by diplomacy" seduce her husband with wiles of "sense and sanity." And so the Degarmo household, one assumes, will soon again be infectiously invaded by the "passionate, tiger-like love" (85) that had existed there before the baby's birth. The marriage is saved. "I guess there isn't much in life after youth is gone" (24), Norma sadly observes; and, through a self-imposed regime of exercises (a program followed by nearly all of Phillips' svelte heroines), Norma warns the American wife to preserve her youth and physical attractiveness—or else. After all, as soon as Norma's waistline had started to expand, hadn't Joe begun to develop an interest in Mazie Bramwell with "her graceful, alluring figure" clothed in "Paris dress—and lingerie ..."? (96).

"Enid" is a story that deglamorizes conventional marriage. Enid Holmes, a pre-Raphaelite damsel "out of a Swinburne or Rossetti poem" (137), marries Walter Prescott, a young executive in his father's stove foundry. They settle into a humdrum marriage near the home office of the firm in Lester, Pennsylvania, where, finally, Enid helplessly wails, "My life is utterly empty" (165). Practical businessman Walter feels that Enid's unhappiness stems directly from her "strange, sensitive nature" and that she must take steps to adjust to the tedium of day-to-day existence among the elect in Lester: "Try to interest yourself in your life. I assure you, my dear, no matter where you live or with whom, you will find living a practical business. It can't have the hazy, unreal atmosphere of the novels and the poems. Force yourself to be interested, and soon you will be interested without forcing. There's nothing in brooding or cloud and rainbow-chasing.... Poets get up that sort of stuff—not to live, but to *sell* ..." (183).

When Enid declares that she cannot live "a crude, unimaginative life," her husband firmly urges her to "try it" for one "can't live on air" (184). So a business arrangement is made: Walter supplies the money; Enid does the housekeeping. When she visits her cousin Jennie, there is a contrast between the roles of these two young housewives: Jennie is a plaything whose job is "keeping bathed and dressed and perfumed and pretty and sweet" (199); Enid is a servant who can "qualify as a housekeeper" (200). The depressive result: Enid Holmes Prescott becomes "hopelessly practical" and settles down in her "soberly furnished" home (232). She loves her husband—not with a feeling she would have experienced in her "poetry and novel days" but with a "comfortable" domestic content. Earlier she had confided to Jennie the hollow terror gnawing at her very soul: "Sometimes I'm almost tempted to give up hope—

and settle down and be commonplace, like the rest of the women. Never have a dream—or an emotion—or a longing" (205). The poetry and romance, indeed, are over; her dreams are shattered. Enid has "grow[n] to like what [she has] got to like" (230). She is married; the death of imagination must follow.

There are other means, Phillips intimates, to show the decimation of a dream; and Georgina Bristow, heroine of "White Roses and Red," rejected the world of conventional love and disillusion to take "the veil" (326). In love with the aging Robert Fenton ("Now my sword is rusted to the scabbard...." he sighs) in this dramatic contrast of innocence and pessimism, the exuberant girl, "so ethereally beautiful in [the] soft romantic light" is incapable of entering the world of a man who confesses: "My ideals are gone; my enthusiasms are dead—and buried—and forgotten" (317). Only Mrs. Virginia Sylvester, Fenton's long-time "friend," can perceive with sharp pain the demons inhabiting Fenton's limited world; for, in essence, these two experienced social nomads are bound together by some peculiar chain of evil, one that will exclude as an essence of good, the innocent Georgina who is unable, though her purity, to arouse in Fenton the wispy ideal of love her spirit obviously craved. Norma Degarmo and Enid Holmes Prescott learned to adapt their emotional frequency to perceive the practical exigencies of adjustment and living. Georgina refused to consider spiritual compromise; and, having forsaken one ideal, she declined to settle for a lesser dream.

The prodigious energy of David Graham Phillips can be measured not only by the number of his publications but also by the regimen under which he worked. Each morning he was up at five and began to write by six; he went at full speed until noon.[14] While a modern historian notes that Phillips "wrote with the brilliant evanescence of contemporaneity,"[15] there came a series of moments in the novelist's career when he was fleetingly able to unite into a single artistic pattern intuition and the transient American experience. For seven years, at these odd times, Phillips hammered at his plan in a practical workaday routine; and, shortly before his death, he completed the tale of Susan Lenox—a novel that he felt transcended its overt theme

DAVID GRAHAM PHILLIPS

of moral degeneracy and the one that he wished to stand as his monument. Controversial from the day it was first announced, Phillips' *magnum opus*, with its base on a pilgrim's quest after an ever-illusive Dream, is fused from a combination of literary fragments that its author, unfortunately, was capable of modeling and phrasing only one time during his prolific career.

CHAPTER *8*

The Girl That Goes Wrong

O N THE COMPOSITION of *Susan Lenox* David Graham
Phillips bestowed long, painstaking care. As rapidly as he
composed his other novels with an eye toward the quick magazine serial and speedy hardbound publication, so was he with
this special project an embodiment of slow, warm, loving
concern. Begun in 1904, the book was not finished until only a
few weeks before the novelist was murdered. In the midst of
his unbelievable productivity between 1904 and 1911, he often
set aside the project of the moment and returned to *Susan,*
which he had occasionally discussed over the years with Joseph
H. Sears, then head of D. Appleton & Company. Secretive about
the novel, Phillips had advised only that it would "deal with
the sociological side of city life."[1] Early in January, 1911, Sears
was able to read the completed manuscript; and, although the
Appleton executive was apparently disturbed by its "frank sex
revelation," he ordered the story set up in type. By January 22,
Phillips had finished going over the galleys and revising the
final proofs, actually the last he ever examined. His death
obviously threw plans for publishing *Susan Lenox* into a turmoil,
for it was not until November, 1912, that his sister Carolyn
contracted for its serial publication in *Hearst's Magazine.*[2]

There was more delay. The International Publishers, owners
of the periodical, began to have misgivings about their contract.
The number of sensational novels dealing with prostitution and
the white-slave traffic seemed to have suddenly subsided;[3]
bringing out *Susan* might antagonize Anthony Comstock and
the Society for the Suppression of Vice. Finally, the first installment appeared in the issue of June, 1915, nearly four and one-
half years after the author's death. And, if the publishers had

entertained any fearful qualms about Phillips' big novel, there was no evidence of critical squeamishness in the uncontrolled manner *Susan Lenox* was presented. Under the title appeared a critical proclamation that would have delighted the author by its sheer, brassy extravagance: "The greatest American novel ever written. The crowning life work of an American genius."[4]

Nor would he have been displeased by an editorial in the Minneapolis *Journal* that followed hardbound publication in two volumes when the serialization terminated: "Well, Phillips is dead, but his disturbing work lives after him. The work will grow—it cannot do otherwise. It shakes the pillars of society, it is pretty much an indictment of human nature. But it is too strong not to produce its effect. You cannot kill the giants; or move the hills. And America has to its merit one more great book, perhaps the greatest written since 'The Scarlet Letter.'"[5]

I

A hazy legend surrounds the inspirational source of the character,[6] Susan Lenox—an incident that allegedly occurred when Phillips was fourteen years old and saw "a young woman seated in a wagon":

> It was in a western town . . . and the face of the young woman in the farm wagon haunted him long afterward. It was a beautiful face, a face indicating breeding and culture, but it bore the stamp of dumb, hopeless tragedy. As he gazed at her, a gaunt, elderly man, rugged and toilstained, with the hall-mark of the well-to-do farmer plainly legible upon him, climbed to the seat beside her, gathered up the reins, and drove off. Mr. Phillips noticed how the girl shrank and whitened as her companion's shoulder touched her.[7]

Later Phillips learned that a "sordid, notorious, unforgettable" scandal had brought about her marriage to "an illiterate but prosperous farmer." According to the story, the future author became haunted by the look of nobility and suffering upon the face of this woman; it was her pained countenance with its vision of total despair and resignation that remained with Phillips after twenty-five years. He came to use an analogous situation as means of depicting the first physical subjugation of Susan Lenox, the fragile, young beauty of Sutherland, Indiana.

But the major sources and backgrounds for *Susan Lenox* surrounded Phillips from the very day he began his assault on the metropolis of New York and its "apaches." As a journalist who scrutinized police blotters and as a curious researcher who roamed about the city prying into various facets of organized vice, Phillips was made aware of the tenuous and desperate plight of the single woman who was unable to bear the tortures of sweatshop employment. The road to prostitution was easy and well-traveled; for many, the profession was lucrative; for others, it meant desperate survival.

With the passage of the Raines Law in 1896, New York saloonkeepers were permitted to sell liquor on Sunday if they paid a "high" license fee to the state and if they operated a "hotel";[8] that is, an establishment that housed at least ten bedrooms. Quickly "Raines Law Hotels" began to operate: a bar up front and at least ten bedrooms either in back or upstairs. This setup augmented the nefarious scope of prostitution, for these "hotels" did not conflict with the still-flourishing "red-light" districts whose vice-ridden emissaries often ranged from tenement basements to the nearly unassailable heights of respected political office. Flourishing in the slums and existing by wholesale graft, the malodorous decay of New York's promiscuous evil began to pervade the apartments of respectable tenement families. Lincoln Steffens recounted the tale of children as spectators of the infiltration of vice to the Ghetto.[9] A cry for reform swelling in the late 1890's brought into being the Committee of Fifteen, composed of respected leaders of New York in business, politics, and religion, which investigated alleged vice and moral decay and which in 1902, issued its report, *The Social Evil: With Special Reference to Conditions Existing in the City of New York,* a study that gave scholarly documentation to the daily abominations reported in metropolitan newspapers.

Muckraking journals, news periodicals, and novelists alike conspired to keep this inflammatory topic before the eye of the public during the entire literary courtship of Phillips and Susan, his heroine in fiction. One Alfred Hodder, writing for the *Outlook* early in 1903, published startling revelations gleaned from the district attorney's office: in New York there were "almost a hundred thousand women who make their living by prostitution."[10] Hodder affirmed that "the horrors of white slavery in the houses of white prostitution" were not mere "evil fairy tales" but authentic case studies of the social evil as it reached its tentacles into night court and police station to unify the law and the sinner in a massive brotherhood of guilt:

> It may seem almost incredible, the system of supply for houses of ill fame that under the protection of the police has grown up on the East Side, but it exists and it is widely spread. Men put women into houses of prostitution. . . . These men are the so-called cadets. . . . The girl in there has no means by which she can escape. Her clothes have been taken from her: she has perhaps a wrapper, a pair of stockings, and slippers. . . . They are told that they are indebted to the woman of the house . . . and that they cannot leave her without paying. . . . there are several hundred houses in which substantially the same method is pursued.[11]

While honest officials asserted their desire to destroy "all the wretches, cadets, or police officers or politicians, who live on women's shame," the article continued, more sensible would be the elimination of what the Committee of Fifteen had named in its report as the largest single cause of "the social evil," poverty. The Hearst press endeavored to aid in this "war on the Father of Vice."[12] In an editorial titled "Women Who Listen to 'Faust,'" the inevitable subversion of the personality by poverty was emphasized: "Mephistopheles is just as busy with house-maids and poor overworked shopgirls as with any Marguerite that ever lived. And his work is made easier by long hours, dull routine, and hopeless future."[13]

The future of the tenement girl, as Susan Lenox was to learn, lies in Blackwell's Island (prison), Bellevue Hospital, or the morgue: for poverty has placed on the street "thousands" of "miserable women" hopefully walking "on cold Winter nights."[14] Indeed, even in muckraking novels that exposed evils in other areas of American society—Brand Whitlock's *The Turn of the Balance* (1907, prison reform) and Upton Sinclair's *The Jungle* (1906, Beef Trust)—poverty drove beautiful and virtuous working-girls into houses of prostitution. The August, 1905, issue of *McClure's* had carried O. Henry's stinging fictional commentary on shopgirls and slavery in "An Unfinished Story." In it, Dulcie, the heroine who earns five dollars a week in a department store,

this one time has enough physical and moral fortitude to withstand the allurement of a substantial dinner tendered by Piggy,
the cadet, a connoisseur "in starvation" who intuitively knows
which hungry girls would be most susceptible to candidacy for
a Raines Law Hotel or a brothel. The next time, O. Henry
intimates, Dulcie will be just as likely to succumb. He vigorously
cited as chief supporters of the happily succeeding cadet system,
the depraved poverty-makers "who hired working-girls, and
paid 'em five or six dollars a week to live on."

More than four years later *McClure's* was still featuring fiction
dealing with the "social evil": a story called "The Man Higher
Up" by Edward B. Waterworth was an explosive tale of vice,
murder, and suicide; but definite emphasis was on the lurid
relationship between the madam of a "house," Gwendolyn Case,
and the law as represented by a corrupt police sergeant. One
major incident can illustrate the raging sensationalism the tales
of the "red light" district purveyed to American magazine
readers: "Shots rang out as Sergeant Clanahan approached the
house one evening on his nightly round; and as he dashed
through the door, he saw the Case woman, intoxicated and
defiant, looking at the prostrate form of one of her inmates, a
young girl whose face had not become utterly hardened and
whose evening gown was stained with the blood which flowed
from a wound in the breast. 'Tried to get away without paying
what she owed me,' explained the woman hoarsely; 'tried to
get out—.'"[15] David Graham Phillips, with his eye for the
timely and with his intimate knowledge of the "apaches" of
New York City, noted many fictional analogues for the way-
stations depicted in the odyssey of his Susan Lenox.

S. S. McClure and his muckraking journal, however, circulated
more than melodramatic fiction in the crusading publisher's
effort to expose the social distemper of the times. One of his ace
muckrakers, George Kibbe Turner, had in April, 1907, written
a shocking article titled "The City of Chicago: A Study of the
Great Immoralities," which revealed the "criminal saloon" and
turned the national spotlight of reform on the "350 good-sized
houses of prostitution" in the city and the "4,000 women"
affiliated with them.[16] A Vice Commission established to investigate this condition concluded that poverty, among sweatshop and department store girls, afforded cadets an accessible

field for recruiting. But New York, in the long run, was Turner's major target. The vast extent of prostitution and the types of women plying this trade were the open secrets of an entire city.

By 1908 the situation had reached the Broadway stage with Eugene Walter's drama *The Easiest Way: An American Play Concerning a Particular Phase of New York Life*. In it Laura Murdock, a "kept" woman, is prophetically told by the manly Westerner who would make her "honest": " 'With you it is the easy way, and it always will be. You'll go on and on until you're finally left a wreck, just the type of the common woman. And you'll sink until you're down to the very bed-rock of depravity. I pity you.' "[17] The play closes with Laura throwing on a "flashy dress," humming a "rag-time melody ... peculiarly suggestive of the low life, the criminality and prostitution that constitute the night excitement of that section of New York known as the Tenderloin," and defiantly announcing: "I'm going to Rector's to make a hit, and to hell with the rest."

Thus when in the November, 1909, issue of *McClure's* both Turner and his editor aimed a double-barrelled volley at the morals of the city, people were startled to see documented the conditions they had suspected for many a day; for both Turner and McClure placed the blame on Tammany Hall. Turner's study, "The Daughters of the Poor," purported to give "a plain story of the development of New York City as a leading center of the White Slave trade of the world";[18] and S. S. Mc-Clure examined this malady as "The Tammanyizing of a Civilization."[19] Both authors drew heavily on the report of 1902 tendered by the Committee of Fifteen: "cadet" was defined, and his inhuman recruitment of immigrant girls, who from sheer loneliness stopped for a moment of pleasure at a Dancing Academy, was chronicled in terms to arouse heated anger and disgust. There appeared to be a vast conspiracy among employment agencies, benevolent associations, local "toughs," and slum politicians to make lower New York City the national center for mass licentiousness—"first" in "the trade of procuring and selling girls in America."[20] McClure discussed the Raines Law Hotel (often "managed by ward syndicates"), the drugging of unsuspecting innocents, the system of the "protector" who stood between the prostitute and the "fly cop," and the "powerful madame," who was capable of conducting a "reign of terror" among the "honest patrolmen."

The indignant charges of these muckrakers could not be ignored, and on January 3, 1910, the Honorable Thomas C. O'Sullivan, Judge of the Court of General Sessions of New York, charged an Additional Grand Jury, headed by John D. Rockefeller, Jr., to investigate the "White Slave Traffic."[21] And, while the jury in its report exonerated the alleged "incorporated syndicates" and "international bands" of being engaged in this commercial trade, the Rockefeller group did assert "that a trafficking in the bodies of women does exist and is carried on by individuals acting for their own individual benefit" in "informal association."[22]

Shocking statements from the Committee that could not be set aside as muckraking excess or as magazine fiction included corroborative proof that agents of the jury "purchased" girls for houses at a price range of sixty to seventy-five dollars; that some 125 beauty parlors were "equipped for illegitimate purposes"; and that many houses were located adjoining "moving picture shows" to facilitate assignations and recruiting.[23] Obviously, the jury did not conclude—as did Turner and McClure—with a demand for a Tammany ouster; nor was there mention of the conditions among woman wage-earners that made implementation of income a necessity for life. More rigid law enforcement seemed a righteously acceptable answer to the entire moral dilemma.

These bizarre charges and reports, investigations and allegations were in the air of the times. It is inconceivable to think that Phillips was anything but enthralled at the fictional possibilities implicit in the sexual and criminal excesses surrounding him in downtown New York, only short walking distances from his Gramercy Park apartment. By the summer of 1910, in the wake of the widespread interest in white slavery, Phillips came back to *Susan Lenox*. He had, however, dawdled so long that his literary thunder was stolen; for, in August, Reginald Wright Kauffman, a Socialist and an editor of *Hampton's Magazine*, the journal endeavoring to "expose [evil] *calmly* and *truly*," [italics mine][24] brought out *The House of Bondage*. By January, 1911, when Phillips was putting final touches to the galleys of

Susan, Kauffman's novel was into its fourth printing; by April, 1912, it had gone through sixteen printings.[25]

What must have muted Phillips' joy in Susan Lenox and her fictional travails was that Kauffman's Mary Denbigh underwent many similar experiences, but the melodramatic *House of Bondage* brought the unfortunate heroine to disease and degradation and left her in ruins. Mary had begun her journey to Gehenna as a small-town innocent lured away from an unhappy home by a roving cadet who promised her marriage. Taken to New York, she was drugged and imprisoned in the house of Rose Legere. She escaped after a time, but found a metropolis of poverty about her; she walked the streets to live and became allied with a "protector" to avoid being "pinched" by "fly cops" (380). The trade of "hard hours, hard walking, and hard drinking" (381) began to tell on this erstwhile fresh country girl; Mary's gaudy clothes—a necessity for her—became tattered. Frozen and diseased, she was finally reduced to wrapping herself in newspapers "gathered from the gutter" (433). She wandered about Chinatown and was soon an opium addict. Her fringe involvement in a murder drove her to seek the refuge of her Pennsylvania home; she was expelled as a "bad woman." She tried to return to the house of bondage; but, because of Mary's condition, even Rose Legere decided to have nothing to do with her. And on this dismaying note the book ends, frankly lurid with yellow sensationalism, but with enough truth of the common-place to brand its author as more than a fright-monger. "I have written only what I have myself seen and myself heard, and I set it down for none but those who may profit by it," Kauffman insisted in an opening "caveat." He concluded Mary's lesson: "... wherever walked the great god Poverty, that great god led Prostitution by the hand" (405).

The stage was clearly set for the tale of another Mary Denbigh, who, having been ground into the most decadent immoralities of the age, can this time find a persistence of strength and courage to rise above frail, sinful humanity. But for the assassination of David Graham Phillips, *Susan Lenox: Her Fall and Rise* would have followed directly on the heels of Kauffman's novel and fulfilled the Romantic imagination of literary devotees who could exult in a woman's ultimate "triumph."

II

Susan Lenox, whose mother, refusing to reveal the name of her child's father, died as the baby girl was delivered, was reared by her aunt and uncle in a small Indiana town on the Ohio River. The townspeople are conscious of her "bad blood"; and, as she grows into a beautiful sixteen, everyone is silently convinced that eventually she will have "to suffer for her mother's sins." When she innocently attracts a beau from her cousin Ruth, ugly suspicion begins to hover over the household. When Susan, while visiting her mother's grave, accidentally meets this beau in the cemetery, she returns home to be unjustly branded as "loose" in the manner of her mother. In anger and frustration she flees to Cincinnati; her foster parents regard this flight as proof positive of Susan's moral defection. She has permitted a young man to take "liberties" with her. She must be married, quickly ("We ain't going to have any more bastards in this family." [I, 39]). Her uncle returns the numb and dazed Susan from Cincinnati and arranges for an immediate marriage between his niece and hard-working farmer Jeb Ferguson, who happily carries his virgin bride to his shack where he cavorts among the "multitude of fat flies." An animal of the field, Jeb has as major concerns gluttony and sensuality: "He used his knife in preference to his fork, heaping the blade high, packing the food firmly upon it with fork or fingers, then thrusting it into his mouth. He ate voraciously, smacking his lips, breathing hard, now and then eructing with frank energy and satisfaction" (I, 154). "... He crushed her. He kissed her with great slobbering smacks and gnawed at the flesh of her neck with teeth that craved to bite" (I, 155-56).

Susan's "bridal bower" becomes an ash-heap of vicious defilement. The vision of her wedding night appears as a phantasm of horror before Susan Lenox many times. The paradox of her "indelible shame" remains a constant affront: "... upon the scene the moon shone in all that beauty which from time immemorial ... filled the hearts of lovers with ecstasy and of devotees with prayer" (I, 160).

She escapes, and with the aid of Roderick Spencer, a Cincinnati journalist, Susan assumes the name and identity of fictitious

Lorna Sackville, actress on a show boat, the *Floating Palace of Thespians,* managed by Robert Burlingham. She becomes a successful ballad singer; but, when the boat is wrecked in a collision, Susan Lenox and Burlingham, with dwindling finances, find themselves in Cincinnati. He contracts typhoid; to help with medical expenses, Susan sells herself for the first time. Her shame is compounded with irony, for Burlingham dies despite her gesture of philanthropy. She is now alone completely.

From the comparative luxury in the home of her foster parents, to the nightmarish Ferguson farm, to the gaudy, haphazard showboat, to the sweatshop travels Susan Lenox. Now, working at a paper-box factory and living with the Brashear family in impoverished circumstances, her life is again complicated when a fire makes them all homeless. Near famine stalks about. Makeshift families are organized so that workers can pool resources and thus keep shelter and food even scantily available. While Susan and her companion Etta Brashear, "struggling on in chastity" (I, 385), earn inadequate wages in substandard factory lofts, they cannot help but note with envy the "fancy ladies" and "soiled doves" who have escaped tenement life. Hungry, dirty, and disillusioned, the girls take to the street; and their painful misgivings disappear quickly as they enjoy their first meal: steak, vegetables, and beer. Two young men out for a fling live for a few days with Susan and Etta; and, when the interlude is finished, Etta leaves with her "beau" and Susan is alone, but now with some experience and one hundred dollars.

She looks up Rod Spenser, her savior in the Jeb Ferguson disaster, who, suddenly drunk with the fantasy of her as inspiration for his art, resigns his job on the *Commercial* and goes off with Susan to New York where he will write plays. Soon after their arrival, one of Spenser's associates suggests that Susan's presence is hampering the talent and career of her lover. Forever noble, Susan drifts out of Spenser's life for his own good. As volume one ends, Susan Lenox is alone in New York with less than twelve dollars.

Susan first works as a model, but she must give herself to buyers as inducement for placing large orders with her firm. She quits after being ravaged by Gideon, a garment-center delinquent who represents a prestigious company. Then she takes to the streets, where she is picked up by a successful "protector," Freddie Palmer: "With the utmost deliberation he gripped her throat with one hand and with the other began to slap her, each blow at his full strength. Her attempts to scream were only gasps. Quickly the agony of his brutality drove her into unconsciousness" (II, 142).

Her name now Queenie Brown, Susan, with Freddie as her "fellow," drifts from one Raines Law Hotel to another, steeping herself in drink and narcotics. She is "pinched." Freddie falls in love with his charge; but, when he tries to carry Susan off, she nearly kills him and makes her escape from the Tenderloin to the Lower East Side where her degradation becomes remarkably accelerated. Drugged by a cheap cadet, she awakens imprisoned in a "house of bondage"; she escapes by frightening the madam with brazen talk about her political allies in high places—but, to her everlasting shame, not before, she had seen several clients while in her narcotized state. Then from saloon to saloon, among "bilkers" (patrons who refuse to pay) and "lobbygows" (thugs who steal the earnings of prostitutes), Susan sinks to the depths of the social order. Now a drug addict as well as an alcoholic, she is driven from a tenement by respectable matrons ("Several women struck at her as she passed" [II, 237]) and must wander about Grand Street and the Bowery when not seeking the exaltation of "Opium's magic." Then, as Susan ponders the inevitability of her ultimate descent, of "abandoning her body to abominations beyond belief at the hands of degenerate oriental sailors" (II, 256), salvation appears in the person of Rod Spenser, now a drunken derelict whose failure as a playwright has brought about his physical collapse and moral deterioration. Susan is gratuitously presented with "Something to live for—someone to redeem" (II, 262).

Events begin to move with incredible swiftness. On the spot, Susan renounces liquor and opium. She nurses Spenser and pays his hospital bills. They take up their former relationship, each vowing to make a comeback. Through Spenser's associates in the theater, Susan meets Robert Brent, famous playwright and director, who makes Susan his protegé and begins to tutor her for the stage. Spenser begins to philander, and soon he and his mistress are separated. But, when Brent suddenly leaves for Europe, Susan, feeling deserted and rejected by this one man she has come to respect, allows Freddie Palmer, who has

achieved wealth and notoriety as a racketeer and politician, to
talk her into an alliance with him. Susan, then, wallowing in
genteel luxury and the scent of the slums far in the past, goes
to Europe with Freddie, who becomes jealous of her longing
for the stage. He comes to hate Brent, architect of Susan's
ambitions, and he ruthlessly has him murdered.

But Susan Lenox is finally emancipated, for bachelor Brent
has left her his estate. Free from the grasp of economic privation,
she dedicates herself to the theater and becomes a successful
actress, "reputed great." Her frightful days of dependence and
slavery have happily come to a close: "Yes, she has learned to
live. But—she has paid the price" (II, 560). Susan Lenox, indeed,
ultimately climbed the ladder that had beckoned many an early
twentieth-century American wayfarer to success; she accomplished this ascent, however, in a manner that would have been
anathema to Horatio Alger and his holy heroines in the gospel
of hard work. "The wages of sin is death," shouted an earnest
worker for the Salvation Army at Susan Lenox, the streetwalker.
Not so, she retorts: "The wages of weakness is death . . . but the
wages of sin—well, it's sometimes a house in Fifth Avenue"
(II, 196).

III

The theme of *Susan Lenox: Her Fall and Rise* combines
contrasting forces of Freedom and Bondage, for the weary
journey of Phillips' heroine simply reflects her desire to escape
from enslavement. Her brutal initiation into the real universe
launches Susan's pursuit of selfhood into a grimy world run on
a Darwinist timetable. Various instructors in life lecture Susan
Lenox on the philosophy of existence: "For you'll have learned
that only the strong can afford to act at all, and that they can
do right or wrong as they please *because they are strong. . . .*
while you're climbing, no Golden Rule and no turning of the
cheek. Tooth and claw then—not sheathed but naked—not by
proxy but in your own person. . . . you've either got to whip or
be whipped, rob or be robbed . . ." (I, 240, 241, 333).

The cosmic view, furthermore, is straightforwardly Calvinistic:
Susan is forever made to suffer for her illegitimacy, the mother's
shame having clearly preordained the behavior of the daughter;
and Original Sin has bequeathed an unhappy legacy of innate

depravity to mankind: "Don't trust anybody, my dear. The
sooner you get over the habit, the sooner you'll cease to tempt
people to be hypocrites" (I, 267). Susan, through a series of
revelations about life, comes to be initiated into the predatory
world of Hobbesian conflict; in her quest for freedom she
encounters the same forces that motivated Huck Finn's tran-
scendental journey.

The river, too, is Susan's first touch with this sense of freedom;
her serene and easy days on the showboat mark her first success
as a singer, her initial movement toward self-knowledge: "To
the river! That was her destination. And somehow it would be
kind, would take her where she would never, never dream those
frightful dreams again" (I, 167). Susan finds the river possessed
by more than the means for spiritual peace; it can lead her
"away" from the "trackless wilderness" on land.

Much is made, too, of Susan's innocence, isolation, and icono-
clasm—her impulsive, incendiary tendencies ("I'm done with
God!" she cries [I, 68]). Her "isolation," in fact, was the chief
cause of the "extraordinary innocence of her mind" (I, 20), but
the protozoan struggles of humanity hold a terrible magnetism
for her. Susan's isolated innocence fails to cloud her perception
of the evil in humanity; intuitively she knows "the general misery
and horror of the established order" (I, 290). Nevertheless, her
alienation is never used as a means of protesting the spiritual
ethos; rather, she endeavors to adjust to this hell, to collide
with and merge with the blackness of existence. Tempted, she
succumbs every time. Her ultimate freedom will be slavery. The
theater will have accentuated Susan's fundamental isolation by
surrounding her with one-dimensional marionettes of stage door
and hotel. When Susan tells a companion, "I shall always wear
a veil" (II, 152), she is offering a physical symbol of her spiritual
disengagement, as well as acknowledging her sense of sin.

Phillips' heroine actually possesses three separate personalities:
there is Queenie Brown, alcoholic, drug-addicted girl of the
streets replete with police record and cadet; there is Lorna
Sackville, showboat singer, lady of the *demi-monde,* and model;
finally, there is the essential Susan Lenox, a woman who is
strongly possessed by Schopenhauer's pulsating "will to live"
and who with this knowledge can objectively stand aside and
observe her fundamental self being usurped by interlopers

Queenie and Lorna. When Freddie batters Susan and subsequently demands absolute obedience, the tortured heroine
quietly confesses, "I don't do it because I am afraid, but because
I want to live" (II, 144). The real heroine who emerges at the
conclusion of the novel is a genuine amalgam of the three, for
Queenie and Lorna have become immolated in the total personality of Susan. Economic necessity and the dynamic will to
live enabled Susan, in true Darwinist fashion, quickly and
efficiently to become "adapted . . . to her changed surroundings"
(II, 247). She fuses with her environment and measures her
physical resources with uncanny foresight so that on one crucial
occasion, for example, like Frank Norris's Valkyrie Moran, she
vanquishes and nearly murders Freddie in hand-to-hand combat.
And, miracle of miracles, Susan herself steers clear of the hospital
ward. Thus it is not at all remarkable that this woman preserves
her basic innocence throughout this forced march through
Hades. Aloof, by virtue of her schizoid pattern of action, she
herself is not touched by the criminal and promiscuous activities
of her alter egos, Queenie and Lorna. An intrinsic part of her
atavistic past, the primordial call of hunger and cold, the primitive passions of pain and brutality, will be heard by Susan
Lenox as long as she lives. The profile of this famous actress
will suggest "bitterness melting into sympathy" (II, 559).

Phillips was also concerned with stressing what he called "the
irresistible pressure of economic forces" (II, 124). The poverty
depicted in Susan's wanderings about New York City contains
the emotional fervor of Charles Edward Russell's heated
muckraking verses of life on the Lower East Side. Susan's tenac-
ity enabled her to surmount "cheap food in cheap lard, coarse
and poisonous sugar, vilely adulterated coffee, doctored meat
and vegetables" (I, 357). In slum living, weather was more than
a transient annoyance; for every change brought new sickness to
compound the verminized malnutrition prevalent in the most
fortunate tenement situation: "These ghastly creatures crawling
toward the hospital or borne out on stretchers to the ambulance
—these yet ghastlier creatures tottering feebly homeward, dis-
charged as cured—these corpses of men, of women, of boys and
girls, of babies . . . all these stricken ones in the battle ever
waging, with curses, with loud hoarse laughter, with shrieks and
moans, with dull, drawn faces and jaws set . . ." (I, 357-58).

As Susan and a friend are walking near a tenement fire, his "foot slipped on a freezing ooze of blood and slush, and he fell sprawling upon a human body battered and trampled until it was like an overturned basket of butcher's odds and ends" (I, 363). This environment is the reality of the universe; man is by necessity reduced to a raging bundle of basic drives. Queenie and Lorna, exploiters of the sensual, themselves seek only to alleviate their own primitive needs. The compelling passion to escape the slums was as fundamental a drive as sex and food:

> Susan's nostrils were filled with the stenches of animal and vegetable decay—stenches descending in heavy clouds from the open windows of the flats and from the fire escapes crowded with all manner of rubbish; stenches from the rotting, brimful garbage cans; stenches from the groceries and butcher shops and bakeries . . . exposed to the contamination of swarms of disgusting fat flies, of mangy, vermin-harassed children. . . . Sore eyes, scrofula, withered arm or leg, sagged shoulder, hip out of joint—there, crawling along the sidewalk, was the boy whose legs had been cut off by the street car; and the stumps were horribly ulcered. (II, 331)

Suffering to rise from such hideous desperation, Susan cannot feel "shame" for herself as a prostitute. Her philosophic rationale coincides directly with her dynamic "will to live"; she simply states, "You know that nobody can live without getting dirty" (I, 462).

The intellectual ethos of the novel is formed by Robert Brent, who is spokesman for David Graham Phillips and whose words focus on a core of stability that serves to anchor Susan Lenox more to twentieth-century reality than *fin-de-siècle* melodrama. Brent's entire relationship with Susan is in direct violation of Hawthorne's "unpardonable sin"; like Dr. Rappaccini, Robert Brent makes Susan the subject of an experiment and throughout their association his demeanor is one of persistent coldness: ". . . you've acted toward me as if I were a mere machine that you were experimenting with," Susan charges her teacher. "And so you are," is his discouraging retort. Freely admitting that he does not regard Susan "as a human being" (II, 371), Brent reveals a total, all-consuming dedication to his craft; his love is his work. As a man of the world, however, he lectures Susan on politics and art:

Under this capitalistic system the whole working class is degraded.... It's shallow twaddle or sheer cant to talk about the dignity and beauty of labor under this system.... It is ugly and degrading. The fools or hypocrites who talk that way ought to be forced to join the gangs of slaves at their tasks in factory and mine and shop, in the fields and the streets. And even the easier and better paid tasks, even what the capitalists themselves do—those things aren't dignified and beautiful. Capitalism divides all men—except those of one class—the class to which I luckily belong—divides all other men into three unlovely classes—slave owners, slave drivers, and slaves.... Most human beings ... have to be in the slave classes.... They have to submit to the repulsive drudgery, with no advancement except to slave driver. As for women—if they have to work, what can they do but sell themselves into slavery to the machines, to the capitalists. (II, 480-81)

What enables Brent to escape the wage slavery of American capitalism is "talent"; thus will Susan also come up from slavery to economic liberation, the only kind of freedom for which she strives: "How superior to the great mass of your fellow beings who must slave or starve, because they have no talent!" Brent gloats to her (II, 481).

Like many a Phillips hero, Brent is a platitudinarian with a tendency to reduce art and society to an absurd series of propositions revolving about good health, hard work, and genteel taste: his charge must exercise, be submissive to his teaching, and wear acceptable perfume ("sensual without being slimy" [II, 300]). Brent furthermore propounds a truism for Susan on her journey: the theatrical world is an escape from economic privation for the destitute and a release from spiritual bondage for the small-town youth with imagination, sensitivity, and talent beyond the characteristic scope of his neighbors. Susan, then, through Brent and his pedestrian realism, will win by endurance and default. She will win her hollow triumph through suffering because life has run out of hazards for her to confront.

At one point in the narrative, Susan Lenox, like Emile Zola's Gervaise Macquart of *L'Assommoir* and like Norris' McTeague, peers out a hotel window into the street. Rain has just washed down upon the Lower East Side. As she watches the futile parade of humanity, the girl is not struck by a sense of its

nobility or of its propensity to endure. Rather she becomes
overwhelmed by a complete sense of sterility and weakness:

> The rain had once more ceased. Through the gray dimness the
> men and women, boys and girls, on the way to the factories
> and shops for the day's work, were streaming past in funeral
> procession. Some of the young ones were lively. But the mass
> was sullen and dreary. Bodies wrecked or rapidly wrecking by
> ignorance of hygiene, by the foul air and foul food of the
> tenements, by the monotonous toil of factory and shop—mind-
> less toil ... that distorted the body and enveloped the soul in
> sodden stupidity ... [and] meant the breeding of desires for
> the luxury the shops displayed, the breeding of envy and ser-
> vility toward those able to buy these luxuries. (II, 224)

Susan is "fascinated by this exhibit of the price to the many of
civilization for the few." The common denominator both of flesh
and spirit is money. The pervasiveness of materialism, then, is
the lesson preached, at length, by Robert Brent and David
Graham Phillips; and Susan Lenox becomes the intellectual
beneficiary of each. Deserted and degraded Gervaise, inert and
stupid McTeague are predecessors of the disillusioned woman
looking through the glass out onto humanity. But Gervaise and
McTeague are, at last, broken by life. Susan, though mutilated,
is pliant. Sight of the rain has cleansed and baptised her; she
scurries about her room cleaning her apparel; she makes herself
"fresh enough to be new" (II, 223). She finally learns to be
disengaged from the "dreary and sullen" stream of mankind.
Brent has initiated Susan into the cult of the talented and made
it possible for her to dwell among the anointed.

IV

The mixed reception of *Susan Lenox: Her Fall and Rise* was
polarized. Few critics remained unmoved, one direction or the
other, by the novel; and the comments issuing from newspaper
and periodical sources were generally epitomes of extravagance.
Current Opinion for April, 1917, noted that "David Graham
Phillips tunnelled his way through the lowest soil of American
life, and when he emerged on its heights with the tales of
what he saw, the greatest of all these is embodied ... in 'Susan

Lenox,' said to be the 'Uncle Tom's Cabin' of New York's under-world."[26] A Dr. Frank Crane went beyond comparing Phillips' novel in social significance to *Uncle Tom's Cabin* and in literary power to *The Scarlet Letter*. Asserted this critic: "In the four-teenth century Dante Alighieri shocked his dull time by a walk through hell. 'Susan Lenox: Her Fall and Rise' is a trip through modern, American, twentieth century hell. It is vastly more vivid than Dante because the people are the kind with which we are familiar."[27]

Isaac Marcosson, writing in the *Bookman,* found several points of analogy for Susan. Both she and Hester Prynne were "of the Sisterhood of the World's Condemned." Susan, like Bunyan's allegorical entity, symbolized "the Progress of [a] Twentieth Century Pilgrim through the Valley of Experience to the Summits of the Sun." Her entire story "moves with the majesty of a Wagnerian Cycle; it expresses in print everything that symbolic music transmutes."[28] Nor is the critic satisfied until he has wrung out a favorable comparison of *Susan Lenox* and the "Book of Books."

But, such glowing eulogies failed to influence those who felt that the posthumously published masterpiece of David Graham Phillips abounded in dubious hyperbole and in unintentionally riotous humor. Mr. J. T. Gerould posed some considerations in the *Bellman:*

> That Mr. Phillips was sincere I do not doubt, but that he had any intimate knowledge of the life of the young girls who fill our factories and our shops, I do not for a moment believe.... The conclusion of the story is merely laughable. That a woman so sodden with vice, so soaked with whiskey and at last with opium, should escape all its physical penalties, and, without previous apprenticeship, become, almost in a day, a famous actress, contradicts every human experience.[29]

The Boston *Transcript* described the pilgrimage of Susan as "an extremely offensive addition to the literature of pornography."[30] While the author's "consistent exaggeration of the difficulties of women in industry and a humorously romantic view of prostitution" were belabored, *Susan Lenox* was finally appraised by the *New Republic* as "a story that moved ... deeply ... [and] the best thing he [Phillips] ever did."[31]

It was, however, the New York *Times* that directed strongest fire on the novel by branding it "essentially false" and "profoundly immoral" in its treatment of reality:

> False as it is to life in its theory and plan, although in its specific pictures of many of the conditions of life among the very poor it is often sadly true, the story is also repulsive to the last degree. Its long-drawn-out-pages . . . are about as interesting as the report of a vice commission. . . . And it is deplorable that Mr. Phillips's name and reputation should be besmirched by the mistaken posthumous publication of a work of such outworn and conventional falsity and of such thoroughly vicious romanticism masquerading as realism.[32]

When John S. Sumner of the New York Society for the Suppression of vice "called particular attention to about 100 pages in the book which he characterized as obscene matter,"[33] it was evident that Phillips' novel was also attracting the attention of righteousness in high places; and, to a practical publisher who wished to avoid public "scandal," Sumner's views were worth serious attention. The entire objectionable first edition was withdrawn and a "deleted" version brought out. By the standards of today, however, the entire work is tame.

Susan Lenox: Her Fall and Rise, as the *Times* suggested, reads in part like a report from the Committee of Fifteen; documentation of the mores, the language, and the values unifying a portion of the lower depths of metropolitan civilization shows Phillips in his familiar role of social historian. His sharp powers of observation are apparent in every episode, from the painstaking recall of street and place names to the revealing activities of cadet and fly cop. Phillips the journalist reached his apotheosis in this posthumous novel, but it was truly far from the triumphs of Zola, Balzac, and Daudet in their treatments of spiritual profligacy and corruption.

Essentially, *Susan Lenox* was too much a product of times when American readers demanded for their dollars more than a grain of escapist romance and at least a conclusion pointed toward the "smiling aspects of life." Phillips' novel is more of a guide—a rather bizarre one—to the byways of back-alley vice when "fallen women" and "scarlet ladies," cloaked in the mysteries of sin, roamed dark streets as wanton animals and haphazardly seduced incredulous country boys, perhaps like Phillips himself, who had just come to the city. He had again endeavored to exploit a contemporary theme of considerable notoriety and had written a two-volume novel styled as another tract of depravity—but one with a coda of redemption through strength and salvation by talent.

In defense of the novel, however, the excesses of *Susan Lenox* arise only from the distorted view of life Phillips presented as coming from *les misérables* of the abyss whose existence he followed and analyzed. More than a report of the Vice Commission, Phillips' work, because it is fiction, purveys without statistics but with vitality a drama of the times that probes not only a real problem of an epoch but also the spirit of a people.

CHAPTER *9*

The Memoirs of an American Citizen

IN MAY, 1903, David Graham Phillips contributed to *Success* an article titled "Great Magazines and Their Editors." The study has no startling significance in itself, but by analyzing Phillips' stated requirements for publishing a popular periodical one may clarify certain literary proclivities and limitations that were eminently relevant to his own achievement in American letters. As an author, Phillips had a practical grasp of the economics of publishing; he frankly correlated sales with success and concluded that no sensible editor could alienate himself from the public taste and be a "Brahmin, sensitive to caste and condition."[1] He believed that people would buy periodicals whose ideas, written in the general public vocabulary, followed the conventional trend of public opinion. Such a powerful combination of force would assuredly attract the most important patrons of the magazine, advertisers: "To get the advertising at good rates, there must be circulation; and to get circulation there must be popularity; to get popularity, there must be careful consideration of the public tastes and capacities. That means that no editor dares to be a Brahmin, supersensitive about his own caste, or the caste of his contributors, or the caste of his readers."[2] An absurdly candid formula it was, perhaps, but cold-blooded in its facile simplicity for coming to grips with the concept of success in a hotly competitive area of the professional literary market place.

Phillips always followed such a *reductio* series of steps in formulating his own approach to any problem, philosophical or literary. While his works in part bear intellectual resemblance to ideas one notes as having originated in Nietzsche (the female breeder and the male superman), Schopenhauer (the will to live), Darwin (science and society), and Spencer (the futility of reform), Phillips was closer in allegiance to the cracker-barrel thinkers and corn-belt intellectuals who captivated late-nineteenth and early-twentieth century American audiences with the sagacity of Populism: George Horace Lorimer, Elbert Hubbard, and Albert J. Beveridge. These oracles, along with the editorial writers of metropolitan dailies, were the mentors who provided the philosophical substance that Phillips drew from most. Prolific as these admired sages, Phillips by industry could not overcome the lack of a sensitive imagination that blighted his, and their, ability to fuse language and symbol.

One of the more interesting aberrations of Phillips' literary plan was the seeming paradox of his veneration and reverence, simultaneously, for the robber-baron as a deified captain of industry and for the insistent revolutionary as a Socialist who might wish to invert the order of "the system." Yet, Elbert Hubbard, whose "A Message to Garcia" was regarded as a prose-poem of rugged individualism, could write on the pages of his magazine "Yes, I am a Socialist"[3] and five months later deliver a eulogy to James J. Hill: "The man who has the superintendence of ten thousand men."[4] There was, indeed, in David Graham Phillips, too, a grudging admiration for the individual who followed the frontier virtues of honesty, thrift, and work, whether these holy traits led to the dangerous precipice of political radicalism or to the stable purlieu of a seat on the Stock Exchange. Because he was consistently observing the public on parade, the intellectual incubation of a typical Phillips novel might last as long as a rapid perusal of the late city edition. While he exhibited much contempt in his books for the conventional Romancer and purveyor of "hearts and flowers," as he scornfully termed the genre,[5] he freely and happily poached on the abundant preserve of these popular scribblers in his own strong efforts to achieve their sales; he longed for the stature, of George Barr McCutcheon, Gene Stratton Porter, and Harold Bell Wright.

The talent of David Graham Phillips, however, superseded sentimental maunderings about a mythical kingdom or the limberlost. Phillips was capable of writing action; and, while his emotional focus was often disoriented by sentimentality, he revealed a strong ability to chronicle with the eye of a knowing reporter the American vision of reality in his time. Phillips, possessing an unbounded faith in progress and in man's perfectionism because of his own self-made efforts, presented a series of fictionalized case-studies examining the effects of avarice, duplicity, sensuality, honesty, philanthropy, and love among a people emerging from the *mal-du-siècle* of an old century. Surface Realism and melodramatic Romance were the chief ingredients Phillips mixed in his gallery of life: there are no memorable moments of horrible self-confrontation in his work; nor are there moments of spontaneous humor. The limitations of his precinct are encompassed, as he realized, in the daily papers. These sheets, however, preserve for any age an embalmed chain of events intrinsic to the permanent records of an era.

As one of his critics suggested when Phillips turned his wrath against corruption, vanity, and sham in contemporary society, he fell far short of the boldly satiric Roman bard Juvenal, whose withering excision of the Empire, its people, and its follies preserved into modernity the rash tempo of his civilization. Nor can one reliably place Phillips in the tradition begun by Theophrastus and reinvigorated by early seventeenth-century English "character writers" like John Hall, Sir Thomas Overbury, and John Earle; for these microcosmographers mixed insightful observations and virulent satire with a brilliance of wit Phillips never approached.

David Graham Phillips is a critical cipher. No one coterie is satisfied with his ultimate literary performance; for, to his misfortune, he appears to have attracted a set of negative critical labels. Historians regard him with suspicion because he wrote fiction; novelists pay him little attention because of his close alliance with journalism. And to journalism he was a renegade. Even Amory Blaine, F. Scott Fitzgerald's eager undergraduate at Princeton, was ashamed to confess to his intellectual comrades that he had never read Stephen Phillips but that he had "heard" of "the late David Graham."[6]

One must look at the movement of time during Phillips' productive years to discern the true pattern of his thought and contribution. In Hubbard's magazine for May, 1908, Fra Elbertus published a satiric advertisement in which he listed the most prominent character types in America during this high point of Phillips' literary activity:

THE ANNUAL PHILISTINE CONVENTION will occur at East Aurora, Erie County, New York, July First to Tenth, inclusive. On this Happy Occasion representatives of the following Frats, Clubs and Cults are especially invited to be present:

Undesirable Citizens	Multi-Millionaire Robbers	Milksops
Filthy Little Atheists	Commercial Highwaymen	Dirty Infidels
Paid Prevaricators	Holders of Ill-Gotten Gain	Predatory Rich
Mollycoddles	Nature Fakirs	Hired Scribblers
Subsidized Writers	Muckrakers	Liars
Rich Malefactors[7]		

An epigraph on the front cover of the issue presented a surrounding ethos for the "characters of virtues and vices" tendered the ironic invitation: "Give Us This Day Our Daily Work." In capsule form, one might find here the blend of humanity surrounded by the limited arc of David Graham Phillips' literary concentration. Faithful to a muse of functional Realism in sketching the mechanics of his microcosm, and devoted to the machinery of Romance in analyzing the motives and drives propelling his fictional world, Phillips was a laureate of the times. He chanted the clichés of "rugged individualism." He clamored for the abolition of political abuse and poverty. He maintained a belief in the American cult of Perfectionism, seminal to the experience of nineteenth-century followers of Emerson. In his time, however, Phillips felt the responsibility of broadcasting the surge of Darwinism then circulating so freely in the intellectual ether; but he chose to escape some of its more grievous implications through the tempering means of Romance. To study his fiction is to have recreated a tumultuous segment of the American past—and to see unmasked an American writer whose quest for literary eminence drove him to assume, albeit not without question, the pedestrian values of his audience.

Notes and References

Chapter One

1. Alfred Kazin, "Three Pioneer Realists," *Saturday Review of Literature,* XX (July 8, 1939), 4. Phillips is treated with Frank Norris and Robert Herrick.
2. Isaac F. Marcossen, *David Graham Phillips and His Times* (New York, 1932), pp. 305-6.
3. "David Graham Phillips: A Twentieth-Century Novelist of Democracy," *Arena,* XXXV (March, 1906), 258.
4. Marcossen, p. 282.
5. Louis Filler, "Murder in Gramercy Park," *Antioch Review,* VI (Winter, 1946-1947), 504.
6. New York *World,* January 25, 1911, p. 3.
7. "David Graham Phillips: A Tribute," *Susan Lenox: Her Fall and Rise* (New York and London, 1917), I, v.
8. John Curtis Underwood, *Literature and Insurgency* (New York, 1914), p. 183.
9. Marcossen, p. 10.
10. *The Second Generation* (New York, 1907), p. 33.
11. Rupert Hughes, "David Graham Phillips: His Biography," *Book News Monthly,* XXV (April, 1907), 507.
12. Eric F. Goldman, "David Graham Phillips, Victorian Critic of Victorianism," in Willard Thorp (ed.), *The Lives of Eighteen from Princeton* (Princeton, 1946), p. 319.
13. Marcossen, p. 16.
14. Goldman, p. 319.
15. Marcossen, p. 18. Frontier adventure as well as big-city crime was made available to Phillips in this surreptitious reading matter.
16. Goldman, p. 320.
17. Marcossen, p. 17.
18. Anna S. Walling, "David Graham Phillips: The Last Years of His Life," *Saturday Evening Post,* CLXXXIV (October 21, 1911), 19.
19. Marcossen, p. 13. An "unusual kinship and understanding" existed between brother and sister.
20. *Ibid.,* p. 17.
21. *Ibid.,* p. 227. Isaac F. Marcossen had access to Phillips materials that were apparently turned over to him by Carolyn. While her scrapbook of Phillips' early newspaper writings was destroyed, Marcossen himself did away with all letters passing between Phillips and his sister. When a biographer indulges in self-appointed censorship of this type, it is difficult for succeeding students to know or to ascertain what other documents he might have destroyed as well. His book, unfortunately not at all documented, is the only repository of much basic information on

Phillips, particularly on his early life and his newspaper relationships.

22. Claude G. Bowers, *Beveridge and the Progressive Era* (New York, 1932), p. 406, notes the following: "Before me lies a batch of letters between the sister and her brother's closest friend ... letters too sacred to quote." In the Beveridge Papers filed at the Library of Congress are several letters from Carolyn to Albert J. Beveridge that reveal the depth of feeling and monumental sense of loss she felt at Graham's death. The bereaved woman wrote in 1912, "...I am missing Graham more every day, but how could it be otherwise when he was everything and all. What shall I do when his work has all been published!" One year later she wrote Beveridge of a dream: "I could feel the texture of his clothes, and smell his cigarette, and I was supremely happy." Carolyn looked forward with haunting dread to the day when she would finish negotiations about and editorial chores with her brother's unpublished novels.

23. New York *World*, May 4, 1930, p. 3.

24. *The Great God Success* (New York, 1901), p. 3.

25. *The Princeton Alumni Weekly*, XI (February 8, 1911), 291.

26. Bowers, p. 17.

27. Marcossen, p. 19.

28. *The Cost* (New York, 1904), p. 25.

29. *Ibid.*, p. 27.

30. Bowers, p. 12.

31. *Ibid.*, pp. 24-25.

32. *The Cost*, pp. 252-53.

33. Bowers, p. 164. Marcossen, pp. 36-38, quotes samples of ecstatic eulogia from Beveridge to Phillips on the publication of *Golden Fleece*, *The Master Rogue*, and *The Deluge*: "well-nigh perfect," "life brimming to the cup's edge," and "genius" are typical of the encomiums bestowed.

34. *The Cost*, p. 286.

35. "Albert J. Beveridge," *Dictionary of American Biography*, II, 232. "He believed that the 'Old Guard' leaders cared nothing for the well-being of the masses but were working constantly for the protection of selfish interests...." Thus "Bev" soon became a pariah in his own political party.

36. Albert J. Beveridge, "The Young Man in the World," *Saturday Evening Post*, CLXXVIII (September 30, 1905), 2-4.

37. "Albert J. Beveridge," *Success*, VIII (August, 1905), 526-28.

38. "James McCosh," *Dictionary of American Biography*, XI, 615.

39. *Catalogue of the College of New Jersey–Princeton* (1885-1886), p. 84.

40. Perry Miller (ed.), *American Thought: Civil War to World War I* (New York, 1959), p. x.

41. *Ibid.*

42. James McCosh, *The Religious Aspects of Evolution* (New York, 1890), p. ix.

43. *Ibid.*, p. 61.

44. J. H. Cleveland, "Dr. McCosh's 'Herbert Spencer's Philosophy,'" *Nassau Literary Magazine* (May, 1885), 31.

45. *Ibid.*, p. 32.

46. *The Nassau Herald* (published by the Class of 1887, June 20, 1887), pp. 39, 62.

47. *The Princeton Alumni Weekly,* XI (February 8, 1911), 291.

48. *Record of the Class of '87 Prepared for the Quinvicennial Re-Union* (June 7-11, 1912), p. 46.

49. James Paige, "Chairs of Journalism," *Nassau Literary Magazine* (October, 1886), 208.

50. *The Great God Success,* p. 1.

51. *The Nassau Herald,* p. 62.

52. Marcossen, p. 51.

53. Mabel Collins Donnelly, *George Gissing, Grave Comedian* (Cambridge, 1954), p. 109.

54. George Gissing, *Demos: A Story of English Socialism* (New York, n.d.), p. 134.

55. *Ibid.,* p. 455.

56. *Ibid.,* p. 385.

57. *Ibid.,* p. 384.

58. *Ibid.,* p. 383.

59. "The Penalties of Plutocracy," *Saturday Evening Post,* CLXXVIII (July 8, 1905), 11.

60. Gissing, p. 207.

61. *Ibid.,* pp. 381-82.

62. Marcossen, p. 51. The manuscript of this paper is not located in the Princeton University Library, the most extensive collection of primary Phillips material. Perhaps the paper was lost or destroyed, along with Carolyn's scrapbook and her letters to her brother. Thus the Marcossen biography is the sole source; he reproduces only a small portion.

63. *Ibid.,* p. 52.

64. Gissing, p. 339.

65. *Ibid.,* p. 266.

66. *Ibid.,* pp. 14, 12, 383.

67. *Ibid.,* p. 80.

Chapter Two

1. Marcossen, p. 68.

2. *Ibid.,* p. 69.

3. Charles Edward Russell, "The Message of David Graham Phillips," *Book News Monthly,* XXV (April, 1907), 511.

4. Walling, p. 19.

5. Marcossen, p. 83.

6. Anon., "Phillips's Methods," *Bookman,* XXXIII (March, 1911), 13.

7. Marcossen, p. 78.

8. David Graham Phillips, Sr., to Albert J. Beveridge, April 11, 1891. Beveridge Papers, Library of Congress.

9. *The Great God Success,* p. 17.

10. *Ibid.,* p. 28.

11. Marcossen, p. 114.

12. *Harper's Weekly,* XXXV (February 21, 1891), 142.

13. Lessing, whose correct name was Rudolph Edgar Block, worked for

six years as a reporter on the *Sun*. He turned to writing tales of the East Side Ghetto, its "poverty and frightful sufferings." *Bookman*, XVIII (January, 1904), 468-69.

14. *Harper's Weekly*, XXXV (March 21, 1891), 210.

15. *Harper's Weekly*, XXXV (April 25, 1891), 302.

16. "Degarmo's Wife," one of the late tales brought out in a posthumously published collection of Phillips' stories, treats the identical problem with similar focus and identical language.

17. *Harper's Weekly*, XXXV (May 23, 1891), 390.

18. Don C. Seitz, *Joseph Pulitzer, His Life and Letters* (New York, 1927), p. xvi.

19. *Ibid.*, pp. 138-39.

20. David Graham Phillips, "The Millionaire's Art Primer," *Saturday Evening Post*, CLXXVIII (December 30, 1905), 3.

21. Seitz, p. 440.

22. *Ibid.*, p. 5.

23. Marcossen, pp. 185, 189.

24. *Ibid.*, p. 199.

25. *Dragons in the Road*, Manuscript, The Jacob A. Riis Papers, Library of Congress.

26. Charles Edward Russell, *Bare Hands and Stone Walls* (New York, 1933), p. 241.

27. Phillips, "Millionaire's . . .," p. 3.

28. Marcossen, p. 181.

29. Russell, *Bare Hands . . .*, p. 241.

30. May 12, 1906. "But we know who the muckrakers are," the magazine asserted, and nominated–along with Phillips and Russell–Steffens, Tarbell, Debs, Sinclair, London, and George. Clipping, Charles Edward Russell Papers, Library of Congress.

31. The New York *Evening Call*, October 23, 1908, carried this banner: "Charles Edward Russell Joins Socialists." The story gave a sympathetic account of Russell's career: "He has led the band of writers who have, by their earnestness and ability, aroused the people of the United States to the existing social conditions and concentrated the public mind upon the necessity of remedying these evils." Russell Papers, Library of Congress.

32. *Life*, October 14, 1905, clipping in the Russell Papers. Russell published profusely, but most interesting are three volumes of poetry: *Such Stuff As Dreams* (1901), *The Twin Immortalities and Other Poems* (1904), and *Songs of Democracy and on Other Themes* (1909).

33. Russell, *Obstructions in the Way to Justice:* Address before the Fortieth Annual Convention of the National American Woman Suffrage Association, Buffalo, New York, October 20, 1908 (Warren, Ohio, 1908), p. 13.

34. Russell, "A Little Song for 'The System,'" *Songs of Democracy and on Other Themes* (New York, 1909), pp. 34-35.

35. Russell, "Essex Street: A Bourgeois Excursion," *Ibid.*, pp. 48, 53.

36. Russell, "The Message of . . . Phillips," p. 513.

37. *Ibid.*, p. 512.

38. Phillips, *The Great God Success*, p. 73.

39. *Ibid.,* p. 26.

40. H. E. Armstrong, "The Two Masters," *The Book Buyer,* XXIII (October, 1901), 232.

41. Russell, "The Message of . . . Phillips," p. 512.

42. Albert J. Beveridge, "The Young Man in the World," *Saturday Evening Post,* CLXXVIII (July 1, 1905), 1.

43. Albert J. Beveridge, "The Young Man in the World," *Saturday Evening Post,* CLXXVIII (July 15, 1905), 1. Beveridge contributed a series of articles of this type to the *Post,* all with the same title.

44. *Saturday Evening Post,* CLXXVIII (November 18, 1905), 24. Advertising a work by Charles N. Crewdson, "Common Honesty and Common Sense," the *Post* stressed the "bright" and "clever" aspect of the writing. In the *Post* for June 9, 1906, an advertisement for one of its tales, "An Accidental Plutocrat" by George Randolph Chester, states ". . . there is a laugh in every line and joy in every paragraph."

45. Mary Moss, "Significant Trends in Current Fiction," *Atlantic Monthly,* XCII (May, 1905), 694.

46. Lorimer began to serialize Norris' *The Pit* on September 20, 1902. The *Wall Street Stories* of Edwin Lefevre appeared in the *Post,* as well as other romances of trusts and monopolies and politics by White, Wister, and Webster (*The Copper King* [1902]).

47. *Saturday Evening Post,* CLXXV (August 9, 1902), 12.

48. *Ibid.*

49. *Saturday Evening Post,* CLXXV (September 13, 1902), 12.

50. *Ibid.*

51. *Saturday Evening Post,* CLXXVIII (December 30, 1905), 12.

52. "Another False Alarm," *Saturday Evening Post,* CLXXVIII (February 3, 1906), 12.

53. "That Person!" *Munsey's Magazine,* XXVII (June, 1902), 379.

54. "Garlan and Company: A Wall Street Story," *Success,* V (June, 1902), 356.

55. *A Woman Ventures* (New York, 1902), pp. 197, 215.

56. Russell, in an article called "Titles for Sale," Detroit *News Tribune,* July 26, 1908, suggested an American aristocracy: "grand dukes" of Boston and Philadelphia; "dukes" of Buffalo and Detroit. He also wrote on "False Ambition: The Tragic End of Nearly All International Marriages." Clippings, Russell Papers, Library of Congress. Lorimer's *Post* stated, "American girls are not buying as many titles as formerly, but they are getting more happiness." CLXXVIII (September 2, 1905), 12.

57. "Thursday at Three," *McClure's Magazine,* XX (December, 1902), 145.

58. Marcossen, p. 211.

Chapter Three

1. "The Men Who Made the Steel Trusts," *Everybody's Magazine,* VIII (May, 1903).

2. "Shifting Party Lines: A Look Toward the Future by Way of the Past," *Reader,* V (January, 1905), 166-75.

3. "The New School of Socialism in Europe," *Arena,* XXXIII (March, 1905), 242-50.

4. "The Advance in the Cost of Living," *Success,* VII (May, 1904), 327-29.

5. "The Penalties of Poverty," *Saturday Evening Post,* CLXXVII (June 17, 1905), 4-5.

6. "The Penalties of Plutocracy," *Saturday Evening Post,* CLXXVIII (July 8, 1905), 10-11.

7. "The Making of the City Slums," *Saturday Evening Post,* CLXXVIII (July 23, 1905), 13.

8. "Tom Johnson: A Type of Common-Sense American," *Appleton's,* VII (April, 1906), 457-60.

9. "The Great Baltimore Fire," *Collier's,* XXXII (February 13, 1904), 2-8. Special supplement.

10. "Empire of Rothschild," *Cosmopolitan,* XXXVIII (March, 1905), 501-15.

11. Louis Filler, *Crusaders for American Liberalism: The Story of the Muckrakers* (New York: Collier Books, 1961), p. 234. Friends, who often saw the lights burning late in Phillips' Gramercy Park apartment, observed that he was "pounding away at his old black pulpit" of a stand-up desk. His prolific output astonished the literati: ". . . it is almost impossible to pick up a magazine or weekly or even a daily paper in which there is not something from his pen," marveled "The Lounger" in *Critic,* XLIII (July, 1903), 10.

12. *The Lamp,* XXVI (June, 1903), 429.

13. Benjamin O. Flower, "David Graham Phillips, A Novelist with Democratic Ideals," *Arena,* XXXI (March, 1904), 243.

14. David Graham Phillips, "The Menace of Plutocracy," *Arena,* XXXV (March, 1906), 262.

15. *Outlook,* LXXXI (October 28, 1905), 529.

16. New York *Times Saturday Review,* X (October 7, 1905), 650.

17. *Outlook,* LXXIX (March 11, 1905), 653.

18. Phillips to George Horace Lorimer, Paris, n.d. [1904], Lorimer Papers, Collections of the Pennsylvania Historical Society.

19. Phillips to George Horace Lorimer, Biarritz, n.d. [1904], Lorimer Papers, Collections of the Pennsylvania Historical Society.

20. *Saturday Evening Post,* CLXXV (August 23, 1902), 12.

21. Georgine Milmine, "Mary Baker G. Eddy," *McClure's Magazine,* XXXI (May, 1908), 31.

22. New York *Times Saturday Review,* X (December 2, 1905), 832. A review of *The Reign of Gilt.*

23. Arthur Bartlett Maurice, "Mr. Chimmie Fadden of New York," *Bookman,* IX (May, 1899), 212-15.

24. *Critic,* XLIX (September, 1906), 286.

25. Collections of the Princeton University Library contain the manuscript of *The Fortune Hunter* and show the original title as *Mr. Feuerstein.*

26. *Arena,* XXXIV (December, 1905), 661.

27. Thorstein Veblen, *The Theory of Business Enterprise* (New York: Mentor, 1958), p. 153.

28. *Ibid.*, p. 155.

29. George Kibbe Turner, "The Daughters of the Poor," *McClure's Magazine,* XXXIV (November, 1909), 54.

30. Edwin Markham, "Spinners in the Dark," *Cosmopolitan,* XLIII (July, 1907), 310-14.

31. The Right Reverend William Lawrence, "The Relation of Wealth to Morals," in Gail Kennedy (ed.), *Democracy and the Gospel of Wealth* (Boston, 1949), p. 69. The sermon appeared first in *World's Work,* I (January, 1901), 286-92.

32. David Graham Phillips, "The New School of Socialism in Europe," *Arena,* XXXIII (March, 1905), 250.

33. Anon., "Phillips's Methods," *Bookman,* XXXIII (March, 1911), 9-10.

34. *Ibid.*, p. 10.

35. *The Plum Tree* (Indianapolis, 1905), p. 388.

36. *The Deluge* (Indianapolis, 1905), p. 7.

37. *The Plum Tree,* p. 375.

38. *The Cost* (New York, 1904), p. 399.

Chapter Four

1. Works about the Stock Exchange and its barons of manipulation were appealing to a reading public eager to learn the "truth" about America's Empire Builders. In *The Literary Digest,* XXXII (April 7, 1906), 503, the J. A. Hill Company of New York advertised the Wall Street Library, a set of books in five volumes that included *Stock Speculation* and *The A B C of Wall Street*: "This is a subject which every intelligent American should understand, for the influence of this gigantic money-making machine extends to the furthest corner of the United States.... It shows how financial panics are caused, and how to anticipate them. It exposes various Wall Street fakes...." Novels such as John C. Van Dyke's *The Money God* (1908), Edwin Lefevre's *Sampson Rock of Wall Street* (1907), and Henry M. Hyde's *The Buccaneers* (1905) are only symptomatic of the rash of "business" fiction heaped upon booksellers and readers by literary opportunists of the hour.

2. William L. Riordon (Recorder), *Plunkitt of Tammany Hall: A Series of Very Plain Talks on Very Practical Politics...* (New York, 1963), p. 6.

3. "A List of Important Fiction, The Bobbs-Merrill Company," section affixed to *The Plum Tree.*

4. *Ibid.*

5. *Ibid.* Rice, obviously dazzled by the deific portrait of Scarborough, observed that Phillips was "entirely committed to advocacy of the best things in life."

6. Charles S. Peirce, "The Century of Greed," in Kennedy, *Democracy and the Gospel of Wealth,* p. 91. Originally published in *The Monist,* III (January, 1893), the essay had been titled, ironically, "Evolutionary Love."

7. *Ibid.*

8. Bernard Mandeville, *The Fable of the Bees; or, Private Vices, Public Benefits* (ed. by Irwin Primer; New York, 1962), p. 31.

9. *Ibid.*, p. 38.

10. Riordon, p. 81.

11. Anon., "Chronicle and Comment," *Bookman*, XXI (June, 1905), 342.

12. *Ibid.* Opinion was "divided between" Bryan and Beveridge for the prototype of political archangel Scarborough.

13. *Critic*, XLVI (June, 1905), 564.

14. *Arena*, XXXIII (June, 1905), 633.

15. Elting E. Morison (ed.), *The Letters of Theodore Roosevelt* (Cambridge, 1952), V, 262-69.

16. *Ibid.*, p. 263. Throughout this strong letter Roosevelt uses terms like "disgusted," "contempt," "sordid," "conscienceless," and "falsehood."

17. *Bookman*, XXII (December, 1905), 372.

18. Russell, *Bare Hands . . .*, p. 131. The anonymous reviewer of Lawson's *Frenzied Finance* in the *Outlook*, LXXXII (March 3, 1906), 520, had little respect for this "stock-jobber of the most pronounced type"; asserted he, ". . . for ourselves we prefer to trust somebody else's advice . . . as to the methods and principles we shall adopt in reforming the very actual and widespread evils of corporate greed. . . ."

19. Filler, *Crusaders . . .*, p. 172. While he was "sincerely kindhearted and openhanded," Lawson provoked the public by an occasional indiscretion: publishing, for example, a work entitled *Why Priests Should Wed*.

20. Russell, *Bare Hands . . .*, p. 132.

21. "Frenzied Finance: The Story of Amalgamated," *Everybody's Magazine*, XI (August, 1904), 164.

22. Granville Hicks, "David Graham Phillips, Journalist," *Bookman*, LXXIII (May, 1931), 261. The collections of the Princeton University Library contain the manuscript of an unpublished Phillips novel, *Thoughts of Her*, a work embodying a rather sizeable fragment of *The Deluge*.

23. *Outlook*, LXXXI (December 9, 1905), 887.

24. Filler, *Crusaders . . .*, p. 170.

25. Arthur and Lila Weinberg (eds.), *The Muckrakers* (New York, 1961), p. viii.

26. "The Literature of Exposure," *Independent*, LX (March 22, 1906), 690-91. Filler identifies the author of this article as Edwin E. Slossen, who predicted that "Fifty years from now, when the historian of American literature writes of the opening of this century, he will give one of his most interesting chapters to the literature of exposure, and he will pronounce it a true intellectual force, a vital element in the creative activities of later years" (690).

Chapter Five

1. Russell, *Bare Hands . . .*, p. 142.

2. Anon., "Chronicle and Comment," *Bookman*, XXXIII (March, 1911), 10. Millard, familiar with Phillips' work, might have recalled an article "A Senator of the Old Republic," *Saturday Evening Post*, CLXXV

Notes and References

(April 11, 1903), 13, in which Phillips had written, " 'the interests' [and] the rise of bosses have changed the character of the Senate."

3. *Bookman*, XXXIII (March, 1911), 10.

4. Filler, *Crusaders . . .*, p. 124.

5. David Graham Phillips, *The Treason of the Senate* (Stanford: Academic Reprints, n.d. [1954]), p. 2.

6. *Ibid.*, p. 4.

7. "New York's Misrepresentatives," *Cosmopolitan*, XL (March, 1906), 496. While the entire series was called *The Treason of the Senate*, each installment was subtitled.

8. *Ibid.*, p. 488.

9. *Ibid.*, p. 496.

10 Frank Luther Mott, *A History of American Magazines, 1885-1905* (Cambridge, 1957), p. 494.

11. *Ibid.*

12. "Aldrich, The Head of It All," *Cosmopolitan*, XL (April, 1906), 632.

13. "Left Arm of the Monster," *Cosmopolitan*, XLI (May, 1906), 12.

14. "Chief Spokesman of the Monster," *Cosmopolitan*, XLI (June, 1906), 123.

15. "Confusing the People," *Cosmopolitan*, XLI (August, 1906), 371.

16. "The Rise of Foraker." *Cosmopolitan*, XLI (September, 1906), 527.

17. *Ibid.*, p. 531.

18. *Cosmopolitan*, XLI (May, 1906), 4.

19. Filler, *Crusaders . . .*, p. 236.

20. *Bookman*, XXXIII (March, 1911), 12. Phillips' sudden notoriety "more than doubled his market value as a tale-teller."

21. Russell, *Bare Hands . . .*, p. 143.

22. *Literary Digest*, XXXII (March 31, 1906), 469.

23. *Literary Digest*, XXXII (April 21, 1906), 605.

24. Russell, *Bare Hands . . .*, p. 143.

25. Theodore Roosevelt, "The Man with the Muck-Rake," *Outlook*, LXXXII (April 21, 1906), 885.

26. *Ibid.*, 886.

27. *Ibid.*, pp. 883-84.

28. *The Autobiography of Lincoln Steffens* (New York, 1931), p. 581.

29. Elting E. Morison (ed.), *Letters of Theodore Roosevelt*, V, 268.

30. *Ibid.* Phillips was branded as a prime contributor to a national hysteria.

31. *Ibid.*, p. 571.

32. *Ibid.*, VIII, 959.

33. *Literary Digest*, XXXII (April 21, 1906), 605.

34. *Ibid.*

35. "A Change in the Spirit of Magazine Criticism," *Literary Digest*, XXXII (May 19, 1906), 750.

36. "More Remarks on the Muck-Rakers," *Literary Digest*, XXXII (April 28, 1906), 640.

37. "A Change in the Spirit . . .," p. 750.

38. "More Remarks . . .," p. 640.

39. *Collier's*, XXXVIII (November 17, 1906), 9. The editorial begins: "Why not reform yourself, Mr. Hearst?"

40. Russell, *Bare Hands . . .*, p. 143.

41. *Ibid.*

42. *The Autobiography of Upton Sinclair* (New York, 1962), pp. 118-19.

43. Some time earlier in "The Present Upheaval in France," *Cosmopolitan*, XXXVIII (December, 1904), 123-30, Phillips had suggested that Socialism was the sole political philosophy circulating among the masses.

44. *Arena*, XXXI (April, 1907), 438.

45. *Independent*, LXII (June 13, 1907), 1415.

46. William M. Payne, "Recent Fiction," *Dial*, XLII (May 16, 1907), 314.

47. Phillips, "The New School of Socialism in Europe," *Arena*, XXXIII (March, 1905), 243.

48. *Ibid.*, p. 246.

49. "Other Books by David Graham Phillips," section attached to *The Fashionable Adventures of Joshua Craig* (New York, 1909), 371-72.

50. Advertisement at rear of *The Conflict* (New York, 1911), p. 394.

51. "Lawson and His Critics," *Everybody's Magazine*, XI (December, 1904), 70 (advertising section). The "blaze," contended Lawson, would spotlight "every scoundrel with a mask. . . ." *Frenzied Finance* ran in *Everybody's* from August, 1904, to February, 1906.

52. Filler, *Crusaders . . .*, p. 191.

53. Louis D. Brandeis, "The Greatest Life Insurance Wrong," *Independent*, LXI (December, 1906), 1475-80.

54. Walter Lord, *The Good Years* (New York, 1960), pp. 104-19. The chapter called "The Golden Circus" gives a spirited account of Hyde's various social capers on the expense account of Equitable and its policyholders.

55. Steffens, *Autobiography*, p. 530.

56. Collections of the Princeton University Library.

57. New York *Times Saturday Review*, XII (October 12, 1907), 615.

58. *Outlook*, LXXXVII (October 12, 1907), 309.

59. "Light-Fingered Gentry: A Book Study," *Arena*, XXXVIII (December, 1907), 704.

Chapter Six

1. Harold Frederic, *The Damnation of Theron Ware* (Chicago and New York, 1896), p. 379.

2. Charlotte P. Stetson, *Women and Economics* (Boston, 1900), pp. 1-18. This section, reprinted in Louis Filler (ed.), *Late Nineteenth-Century American Liberalism* (Indianapolis, 1962), pp. 207-18, deals with the unfortunate subjugation of woman who in our society must be "fed by the male."

3. Russell, *Obstructions . . .*, p. 3.

4. Gabrielle E. Jackson, *The Dawn of Womanhood* (New York, 1908), pp. 131-32.

5. Anna A. Rogers, "Why American Mothers Fail," *Atlantic Monthly*, CI (March, 1908), 297.

6. Jackson, *Dawn* . . ., p. 248

7. "A Woman to be Pitied," *Editorials from the Hearst Newspapers* (New York. 1906), p. 306. Brisbane (1864-1936) composed the writings in this collection.

8. "The Cow That Kicks Her Weaned Calf is All Heart," *Ibid.*, p. 315.

9. "Woman's Vanity is Useful," *Ibid.*, p. 326.

10. *Ibid.*, p. 327.

11. *Ibid.*, p. 328.

12. "The American Woman and Her Home," *Outlook*, XCVI (September 17, 1910), 117.

13. "Concerning Respectability–An Inquiry," *The Philistine*, XIX (June, 1904), p. 13.

14. *Ibid.*, p. 14. This article also censures the clothing styles in the pattern of "conspicuous waste"; a woman is "rendered . . . an easy prey for any predaceous Roman in search of female Sabines!" (21).

15. Mrs. Newell Dwight Hillis, "Some Failures of American Women," *Outlook*, XCV (July 16, 1910), 572.

16. *Brann the Iconoclast: A Collection of the Writings of W. C. Brann* (Waco, Texas, 1905), II, 280.

17. *Ibid.*, p. 284.

18. Hillis, "Failures . . .," p. 572.

19. Lloyd Morris, *Postscript to Yesterday* (New York, 1947), p. 52.

20. *Dial*, XLVII (November 16, 1909), 386. Review of *The Hungry Heart*.

21. *Independent*, LXXIII (October 17, 1912), 903. Review of *The Price She Paid*.

22. Phillips to Lorimer, November, 1909, Gramercy Park, Manhattan. Collections of the Pennsylvania Historical Society, George Horace Lorimer Papers.

23. Phillips, "Restless Husbands," *Cosmopolitan*, LI (August, 1911), 420.

24. *Ibid.*

25. *Ibid.*

26. *Ibid.*, p. 423.

27. *Ibid.*, p. 425.

28. Goldman, "David Graham Phillips, 'Victorian . . .,' " p. 324.

29. *Ibid.*, p. 328.

30. Phillips, "The Millionaire's Art Primer," p. 3.

31. Hillis, "Failures . . .," p. 574.

32. "Books by David Graham Phillips," Advertisement attached to *The Conflict* (New York, 1911), p. 394.

33. David Graham Phillips, *The Worth of a Woman* (New York, 1908), p. vii.

34. "The Cow . . . Heart," *Editorials* . . ., p. 316.

35. Lyman Abbott, "The Assault on Womanhood," *Outlook*, XCI (April 3, 1909), 785.

36. "When Will Her Mental Life Begin?" *Editorials* . . ., p. 311.

37. Phillips, *Old Wives for New* (New York, 1908), p. 494.

38. Grant C. Knight, *The Strenuous Age in American Literature* (Chapel Hill, 1954), p. 196.

39. Percival Pollard, *Their Day in Court* (New York and Washington, 1909), pp. 192, 194.

40. Henry Louis Mencken, "The Leading American Novelist," *Smart Set*, XXXIII (January, 1911), 163.

41. Marcossen, p. 307. Throughout the canon of his dubious writings Frank Harris testified to the belief that Phillips was "the greatest American novelist": "I want to say quite certainly that I would rather have written *White Magic* or *The Hungry Heart* or *The Price She Paid* or *A Grain of Dust* than all the novels Kipling and Hardy together have written in the last thirty years." (*Latest Contemporary Portraits* [New York], 1927], p. 24).

42. Marcossen, *Ibid.* The enthusiastic critic even publicized his protégé, David Graham Phillips, in the notorious *My Life and Loves* (New York, 1963), p. 888. Asserted Harris: "Phillips [is] the only one indeed to hold his own with Fielding and Thackeray.... I would rather compare Phillips to Turgenief than to any English writer."

43. *Independent*, LXIV (April 9, 1908), 808. Review of *Old Wives for New*. In keeping with his newspaper research to ferret out plot materials, Phillips apparently discovered a notorious contemporary incident which he incorporated as partial substance of *Old Wives for New*. Stated Charlotte Harwood in "Fiction in a Lighter Vein," *Putnam's* (August, 1908), 621, the "recent divorce and remarriage of a self-made millionaire" formed a basis for the novel.

44. The prototype of Dr. Schulze, the common-sense physician who appears in several of Phillips' novels, was probably Dr. John H. Kellogg, whose sanitarium in Battle Creek, Michigan, was world-famous. Kellogg, whose "Health University" was widely advertised in literary periodicals, believed in the "efficacy of baths," "cheerful living," and vegetarianism. Like Schulze, he stressed diet: "Get the stomach right and you will get the physical man right," he asserted. Kellogg, like Schulze and Phillips, believed in the "application of practical sense to the work of getting well" (*Literary Digest*, XXXII [April 7, 1906], 506).

45. Owen Wister, "The Open Air Education," *Saturday Evening Post*, CLXXVIII (October 25, 1902), 1.

46. "Books by David Graham Phillips," Advertisement in *The Conflict*.

47. Frederic T. Cooper, "David Graham Phillips's Place Among Modern American Novelists," addendum to *The Grain of Dust* (New York, 1911), p. 6. This twelve-page article is appended to the novel in a separate section.

48. *Dial*, XLIV (June 1, 1908), 350.

49. *Dial*, XLIX (October 16, 1910), 289.

50. *Putnam's*, IV (August, 1908), 621.

51. *Outlook*, LXXXVIII (April 11, 1908), 838.

52. *Nation*, LXXXVI (March 19, 1908), 264.

53. Knight, *Strenuous Age . . .*, p. 205.

54. *Dial*, XLVII (November 16, 1909), 386.

55. *Literary Digest*, XXXIX (September 18, 1909), 444.

56. *Nation*, LXXXIX (August 26, 1909), 196.

57. New York *Times Saturday Review*, XIV (August 28, 1909), 511.

58. *Old Wives for New*, p. 58.

59. Mencken, "The Leading American Novelist," p. 163.

60. Advertisement appeared in listing of Grosset & Dunlap publications in Phillips' *The Fashionable Adventures of Joshua Craig* (New York, 1909).

Chapter Seven

1. "Concerning Respectability–An Inquiry," *The Philistine*, XIX (June, 1904), 16-17.

2. Abraham Feldman, "David Graham Phillips–His Works and His Critics," *Bulletin of Bibliography*, XIX (May-August, 1948), 144.

3. New York *Times Book Review*, XVII (October 20, 1912), 612: "It is probable that the late David Graham Phillips wrote this just-published novel a great many years ago." In "The Bribe," *Cosmopolitan*, L (January, 1911), 244-50 and "The Compromise," *Cosmopolitan*, L (March, 1911), 453-66, Phillips dealt with Andy Clarke, an attorney, coming to learn the dubious concessions a successful politician must make. Thus, the author again returned to the arena of government for his fictional materials. In Phillips' "Economic Independence the Boast of Freedom," *Arena*, XLI (January, 1909), 17-19, he had marked out the inner limits of compromise between politicians, the "agents of plutocracy," and idealists, the failures who "divorce morals and practical wisdom" (18).

4. *Dial*, XLVI (April 16, 1909), 264.

5. New York *Times Book Review*, XVI (October 1, 1911), 583.

6. New York *Times Book Review*, XVII (October 20, 1912), 612.

7. New York *Times Book Review*, XVI (October 1, 1911), 583.

8. Phillips to Lorimer, June, 1909, 119 E. 19 (Phillips' Gramercy Park Apartment). Lorimer Papers, Pennsylvania Historical Society.

9. *Nation*, XC (June 16, 1910), 607.

10. *Atlantic Monthly*, CX (November, 1912), 686.

11. *Nation*, XCV (July 25, 1912), 81.

12. *Independent*, LXXIII (October 17, 1912), 903.

13. *Good Housekeeping*, LII (June, 1911), 672-78; LIII (July, 1911), 47-54; LIII (August, 1911), 193-201; LIII (September, 1911), 336-41. "White Roses and Red" was this serialized title. "Degarmo's Wife" was lengthened only in detail from "The First Born," *Harper's Weekly*, XXXV (May 23, 1891), 390.

14. *Saturday Evening Post*, CLXXVIII (March 10, 1906), 17.

15. Goldman, "David Graham Phillips, Victorian . . .," p. 332.

Chapter Eight

1. Marcossen, p. 253.

2. *Ibid.*, p. 254. *Susan Lenox*, because of the delay in publication, was the topic of much literary gossip. Speculated one commentator, "The title of the book has not been made public, but it is probably safe to conjecture

that it is the volume that he intended to call *Susan*" (*Bookman*, XXXIII [March, 1911], 9).

3. George Jean Nathan, "Inside Views of Fiction," *Bookman*, XXXIII (April, 1911), 202-4. Subtitled "The Girl-Alone-in-the-City Novels," the article treats the rise and the inevitable fall of the "voluminously immoral" and "scarlet-crested" fictional hosts of the penniless woman in chains.

4. *Hearst's International Magazine*, XXVII (June, 1915), 482. Titled in the magazine "The Story of Susan Lenox: Her Fall and Rise," the tale was *Hearst's* "greatest box-office success." Mott, *History*, 501.

5. Anon., "The Contested Merits of David Graham Phillips's Posthumous Novel," *Current Opinion*, LXII (April, 1917), 274.

6. *Bookman*, XXXIX (March, 1914), 19. Phillips, so this article tells, first titled his novel *Susan;* then *A Woman of the Streets*.

7. *Bookman*, XXXIII (March, 1911), 9.

8. Filler, *Crusaders . . .*, p. 265.

9. *The Autobiography of Lincoln Steffens*, p. 245.

10. Alfred Hodder, "A Fight for the City," *The Outlook*, LXXIII (January 31, 1903), 254.

11. *Ibid.*, pp. 258-59.

12. "Poverty is the Father of Vice, Crime, and Failure," *Editorials*, p. 235.

13. "Respectable Women Who Listen to 'Faust,' " *Ibid.*, p. 318.

14. "Poverty . . .," *Ibid.*, pp. 235-36.

15. Edward B. Waterworth, "The Man Higher Up," *McClure's Magazine*, XXXIV (February, 1910), 458. O. Henry wrote a tale with the same title, but its theme was totally different.

16. George Kibbe Turner, "The City of Chicago," *McClure's Magazine*, XXVIII (April, 1907), 581.

17. Thomas Herbert Dickinson, editor, *Chief Contemporary Dramatists* (Second Series) (New York, 1921), p. 224.

18. George Kibbe Turner, "The Daughters of the Poor," *McClure's Magazine*, XXXIV (November, 1909), 45.

19. S. S. McClure, "The Tammanyizing of a Civilization," *McClure's Magazine*, XXXIV (November, 1909), 117.

20. Turner, "Daughters," p. 59.

21. "White Slave Traffic," *Presentment of the Additional Grand Jury for the January Term of the Court of General Sessions . . .*, Proceedings attached to Reginald Wright Kauffman, *The House of Bondage* (New York, 1910), pp. 467-80 (469).

22. *Ibid.*, p. 472.

23. *Ibid.*, p. 476.

24. Harvey Swados (ed.), *Years of Conscience: The Muckrakers* (New York and Cleveland, 1962), p. 409. Reprint of an editorial from *Hampton's Magazine* (September, 1909).

25. Copyright page in Grosset & Dunlap reprint edition of the novel, April, 1912. Despite the enormous notoriety of Kauffman's novel, it fell short of being included in any of Frank Luther Mott's tables of popularity in *Golden Multitudes: The Story of Best Sellers in the United States*

(New York, 1947). Ironically, the best-seller for 1910 was Florence L. Barclay's *The Rosary.*

26. *Current Opinion,* LXII (April, 1917), 274.

27. *Bookman,* XLV (March, 1917), 113.

28. Marcossen, "The Significance of Susan Lenox," *Bookman,* XLV (March, 1917), 31.

29. *Bellman,* XXII (April 7, 1917), 385.

30. Boston *Transcript,* March 3, 1917, p. 6.

31. *New Republic,* X (March 10, 1917), 167.

32. New York *Times Book Review,* XXII (February 25, 1917), 62-63.

33. Marcossen, *David Graham Phillips . . .,* pp. 260-61. The New York *Times,* April 3, 1917, p. 9, told of D. Appleton & Co.'s incipient trial for the "publication or circulation of obscene matter." Sumner was named as complainant. Feeling that the Court would leave a permanently harmful brand upon the book, Sears and Carolyn Phillips Frevert reached a compromise with Sumner, and the "acceptable" version was published, after the withdrawal of the first edition.

Chapter Nine

1. *Success,* VI (May, 1903), 305.

2. *Ibid.*

3. *The Philistine,* XVIII (December, 1903), 17.

4. *Ibid.* (May, 1904), 176.

5. Phillips, "Great Magazines . . .," pp. 305-6. The author made a plea for a fiction of reality based on creative imagination rather than on whimsical fantasy.

6. F. Scott Fitzgerald, *This Side of Paradise* (New York, 1960), p. 50. The original publication date is 1920.

7. *The Philistine,* XXVI (May, 1908), n.p.

Selected Bibliography

MANUSCRIPTS

The Library of Congress: The Albert J. Beveridge Papers, The Jacob Riis Papers, The Charles Edward Russell Papers. The collections of Riis and Russell illuminate the times as seen through the writings of two deeply involved reformers. The Beveridge Papers chronicle a vital segment of Americana as events paraded across the desk of a politician surrounded by our affairs of state. The close friendship of Beveridge with Phillips and his family is revealed.

The Library of the Pennsylvania Historical Society, Philadelphia: The George Horace Lorimer Papers. This collection throws light upon Phillips and his major editor. The literary tempo and focus of the *Saturday Evening Post* come through with strong clarity.

The Princeton University Library: The David Graham Phillips Papers. Drafts of Phillips' novels, stories, and articles are included here. His revisions and methods of composition can be studied in these primarily handwritten papers. The Princeton Archives hold all local publications issued during Phillips' tenure at the university.

BIBLIOGRAPHIES

FELDMAN, ABRAHAM. "David Graham Phillips, His Works and His Critics," *Bulletin of Bibliography,* XIX (May-August, 1948), 144-46; (September-December, 1948), 177-179.

RODGERS, PAUL C., JR. "David Graham Phillips: A Critical Study," Unpublished Dissertation, Columbia University, 1955.

PRIMARY SOURCES

I. *Books*

The Great God Success: A Novel. New York: Frederick A. Stokes Company, 1901.

Her Serene Highness: A Novel. New York and London: Harper and Brothers, 1902.

A Woman Ventures: A Novel. New York: Frederick A. Stokes Company, 1902.

Golden Fleece: The American Adventures of a Fortune Hunting Earl. New York: McClure, Phillips and Company, 1903.

The Master-Rogue: The Confessions of a Croesus. New York: McClure, Phillips and Company, 1903.

The Cost. Indianapolis: The Bobbs-Merrill Company, 1904.

Selected Bibliography

The Mother-Light. New York: D. Appleton and Company, 1905. Published anonymously.

The Plum Tree. Indianapolis: The Bobbs-Merrill Company, 1905.

The Reign of Gilt. New York: James Pott and Company, 1905. Collected essays.

The Social Secretary. Indianapolis: The Bobbs-Merrill Company, 1905.

The Deluge. Indianapolis: The Bobbs-Merrill Company, 1905.

The Fortune Hunter. Indianapolis: The Bobbs-Merrill Company, 1906.

The Treason of the Senate. Stanford, California: Academic Reprints, n.d. 1954. Originally published *Cosmopolitan* (March-November, 1906).

The Second Generation. New York: D. Appleton and Company, 1907.

Light-Fingered Gentry. New York: D. Appleton and Company, 1907.

Old Wives for New: A Novel. New York: D. Appleton and Company, 1908.

The Worth of a Woman: A Play. New York: D. Appleton and Company, 1908.

The Fashionable Adventures of Joshua Craig: A Novel. New York: D. Appleton and Company, 1909.

The Hungry Heart: A Novel. New York and London: D. Appleton and Company, 1909.

White Magic: A Novel. New York and London: D. Appleton and Company, 1910.

The Husband's Story: A Novel. New York and London: D. Appleton and Company, 1910.

The Grain of Dust: A Novel. New York and London: D. Appleton and Company, 1911.

The Conflict: A Novel. New York and London: D. Appleton and Company, 1911.

The Price She Paid: A Novel. New York and London: D. Appleton and Company, 1912.

George Helm. New York and London: D. Appleton and Company, 1912.

Degarmo's Wife and Other Stories. New York and London: D. Appleton and Company, 1913.

Susan Lenox: Her Fall and Rise. New York and London: D. Appleton and Company, 1917. Two volumes.

II. *Other Writings*

Fiction:

"The First-Born," *Harper's Weekly*, XXXV (May 23, 1891), 390.

"Garlan and Company," *Success*, V (June, 1902), 351-56.

"That Person." *Munsey's*, XXVII (June, 1902), 374-79.

"Thursday at Three," *McClure's*, XX (December, 1902), 143-53.

"The Bribe," *Cosmopolitan*, L (January, 1911), 241-50.

"The Compromise," *Cosmopolitan*, L (March, 1911), 453-66.

"The Little Joker," *Cosmopolitan*, LI (September, 1911), 512-21.

Non-fiction:

"The Sioux Chiefs Before the Secretary," *Harper's Weekly*, XXXV (February 21, 1891), 142.

"The Rescue of the Jeansville Miners," *Harper's Weekly*, XXXV (March 7, 1891), 177-78.

"A Senator of the Old Republic," *Saturday Evening Post*, CLXXV (April 11, 1903), 12-13.

"Great Magazines and Their Editors," *Success*, VI (May, 1903), 303-9.

"The Madness of Much Power," *Everybody's*, X (February, 1904), 230-34.

"The New School of Socialism in Europe," *Arena*, XXXIII (March, 1905), 242-50.

"The Penalties of Plutocracy," *Saturday Evening Post*, CLXXVIII (July 8, 1905), 10-11.

"Albert J. Beveridge," *Success*, VIII (August, 1905), 526-28.

"The Millionaire's Art Primer," *Saturday Evening Post*, CLXXVIII (December 30, 1905), 2-3, 20-21.

"Economic Independence the Basis for Freedom," *Arena*, XLI (January, 1909), 17-19.

"What Is a Successful Wife?" *Delineator*, LXXVII (April, 1911), 265-66, 327-28.

"Restless Husbands," *Cosmopolitan*, LI (August, 1911), 419-25.

SECONDARY SOURCES

ARMSTRONG, H. E. "The Two Masters," *The Book Buyer*, XXIII (October, 1901), 230-32. The "masters" are Love and Success in Phillips' *The Great God Success*.

BOWERS, CLAUDE. *Beveridge and the Progressive Era*. New York: The Literary Guild, 1932. Valuable for the Beveridge-Phillips lifetime relationship.

COOPER, FREDERIC TABER. *Some American Story Tellers*. New York: Henry Holt and Company, 1911. "David Graham Phillips," pp. 112-39. Phillips studied the "big ethical and social problems of American life" with a "certain epic sweep and magnitude."

FILLER, LOUIS. "An American Odyssey: The Story of Susan Lenox," *Accent*, I (August, 1940), 22-29. A study of the backgrounds of Phillips' major novel.

———. *Crusaders for American Liberalism*. New York: Collier Books, 1961. Originally published in 1939, this work is the standard treatment of the entire muckraking movement.

———. "Murder in Gramercy Park," *Antioch Review*, VI (Winter, 1946-1947), 495-508. A "weak fantasy... then in vogue," George Sylvester Vierick's novel *House of the Vampire* "formed the inspiration for what became Goldsborough's one obsession."

———. "The Reputation of David Graham Phillips," *Antioch Review*, XI (December, 1951), 475-88. "Yet it is worth considering whether Phillips, walking boldly in the ways of experiment and rude honesty, may not have been blazing a trail for American writers."

Selected Bibliography

FLOWER, B. O. "David Graham Phillips: A Novelist with Democratic Ideals," *Arena*, XXXI (March, 1904), 236-43. A favorable evaluation of "the keen analytical, faithful and fearless stories" of Phillips.

——. "David Graham Phillips: A Twentieth-Century Novelist of Democracy," *Arena*, XXXV (March, 1906), 252-57. Phillips is "foremost in this irrepressible conflict between freedom and despotism, between justice for all and the tyranny of privileged wealth."

GOLDMAN, ERIC F. "David Graham Phillips, Victorian Critic of Victorianism," in *The Lives of Eighteen from Princeton,* ed. WILLARD THORP. Princeton: Princeton University Press, 1946. "Obviously the enthusiasm for Phillips's novels came from the fact that he offered vigorous criticism of the *status quo* to a generation avid for revolt." (322)

HICKS, GRANVILLE. "David Graham Phillips, Journalist," *Bookman*, LXXIII (May, 1931), 257-66. "For Phillips was a good journalist . . . [who] could describe the life of his times with the vigor and explicitness of a star reporter, and that is no mean gift. How many of our novelists from Howells on have fallen down at precisely this point."

HUGHES, RUPERT. "David Graham Phillips: His Biography," *The Book News Monthly,* XXV (April, 1907), 507-10. Brief account of Madison, Indiana, and the essential facts of Phillips' early life.

KAZIN, ALFRED. "Three Pioneer Realists," *Saturday Review of Literature,* XX (July 8, 1939), 3-4, 14-15. The "three" are Robert Herrick, Frank Norris, and Phillips. "It was his [Phillips'] greatest desire to lay bare the debasement of the middle-class spirit in a plutocracy; instead, he succeeded only in documenting, out of the overflowing knowledge he had gained as a reporter, the crucial processes in politics, business and finance."

KNIGHT, GRANT C. *The Strenuous Age in American Literature.* Chapel Hill: The University of North Carolina Press, 1954. A lively account of American letters during the first decade of the twentieth century.

LEWISOHN, LUDWIG. *The Story of American Literature.* New York: The Modern Library, 1939. "Phillips was an awkward and muddy writer . . . yet was he not in truth the first American who made an attempt, at least, to deal honestly with the concrete lives and unvarnished adventures of men and women?" (326-27).

LYNN, KENNETH S. *The Dream of Success: A Study of the Modern American Imagination.* Boston and Toronto: Little, Brown, 1955. "David Graham Phillips, The Dream Panderer," pp. 121-57. "Phillips's novels . . . compose a secret history—not, however, of the private lives of middle-class Americans, but of their private, innermost hopes and dreams."

MARCOSSEN, ISAAC F. *David Graham Phillips: His Life and Times.* New York: Dodd, Mead and Company, 1932. Good for backgrounds in journalism but weak in treatment of Phillips as a novelist.

——. "The Significance of *Susan Lenox,*" *Bookman*, XLV (March, 1917), 23-31. The history and the value of Phillips' novel are treated by an ardent supporter.

McCLOSKEY, JOHN C. "Social Criticism in the Novels of David Graham Phillips," Unpublished doctoral dissertation, Stanford University, 1939. Stress is on Phillips' Darwinism.

MENCKEN, HENRY LOUIS. "The Leading American Novelist," *The Smart Set*, XXXIII (January, 1911), 163-64. Phillips is nominated by iconoclast-editor.

MORRISON, ELTING E. (ed.). *The Letters of Theodore Roosevelt*, V. Cambridge: Harvard University Press, 1952. Documents reveal the attitude of President Roosevelt toward the enigmatic muckraker.

POLLARD, PERCIVAL. *Their Day in Court*. Washington: Neale Publishing Company, 1909. Phillips is given sympathetic treatment, pp. 188-94.

RODGERS, PAUL C., Jr. "David Graham Phillips, A Critical Study," Unpublished doctoral dissertation, Columbia University, 1955. A valuable work that contains much primary material dealing with Carolyn Phillips Frevert, in addition to interviews with individuals who knew Phillips and his family.

RUSSELL, CHARLES EDWARD. *Bare Hands and Stone Walls: Some Recollections of a Sideline Reformer*. New York: Charles Scribner's Sons, 1933. A prime account of the muckrake movement by one of its most effective participants.

————. "The Message of David Graham Phillips," *The Book News Monthly*, XXV (April, 1907), 511-13. A strong endorsement of Phillips as a novelist.

TEBBEL, JOHN W. *George Horace Lorimer and the Saturday Evening Post*. New York: Doubleday, 1948. "Nor could Lorimer stomach the novelist's [Phillips'] later work when he began to examine the changing sexual standards of women." (53)

UNDERWOOD, JOHN CURTIS. *Literature and Insurgency*. New York: Mitchell Kennerley, 1914. "David Graham Phillips and Results," pp. 179-253. "Phillips's moral vivisections are those of the surgeon and scientist. . . . As such he is characteristically American, an intensely modern exemplar and prophet of twentieth century unrest and reconstruction." (251)

WALLING, ANNA S. "David Graham Phillips, The Last Years of His Life," *Saturday Evening Post*, CLXXXIV (October 21, 1911), 19-20. Phillips "was an idealist, as are all radicals."

Index

Index

Davis, Richard Harding, 56
Debs, Eugene, 106, 126
Democracy, 75
Demos, 25-30, 95
DePauw University (*see* Asbury)
Depew, Chauncey M., 83-85, 86
Dial, 94, 115-16, 119-20, 130
Dickens, Charles, 17, 31
The Divinity School Address, 87
Dorothy Vernon, 45
Dostoievsky, Feodor, 111
Dreiser, Theodore, 17, 116
d'Utassy, George, 84

Earle, John, 163
The Easiest Way, 146
Eddy, Mary Baker, 54-55, 110
Ellis, Havelock, 100
Emerson, Ralph Waldo, 87, 164
"Essex Street: A Bourgeois Excursion," 39-40
Esther Waters, 111
Everybody's Magazine, 39, 49, 76, 79, 82, 95

Fitzgerald, F. Scott, 163
Flower, Benjamin O., 15, 51, 74, 95, 99
A Fool There Was, 121
Foraker, Joseph Benson, 85
Franklin, Benjamin, 43
Frederic, Harold, 100
Frenzied Finance: The Story of Amalgamated, 76
Frevert, Carolyn Phillips, 17-19, 31, 32, 42, 141

Gerould, J. T., 158
Gissing, George, 25, 27, 29, 95
Goldman, Emma, 106
Goldsborough, Fitzhugh Coyle, 15-16
Gorman, Arthur P., 85
"Graham, John" (pseudonym), 41
Graustark, 44-46, 131
"The Great Life Insurance Wrong," 96
Grosset and Dunlap, 121
The Grumbling Hive, 73-74

Hall, John, 163
Halstead, Clarence, 24, 30
Halstead, Marshall, 24, 30
Hampton's Magazine, 147
Hanna, Mark, 74
Harland, Henry, 56
Harper's Weekly, 33, 35, 137
Harris, Frank, 110-11
Harte, Bret, 80
Harwood, Charlotte, 116
Hawthorne, Nathaniel, 142, 154
Haymarket Riot, 127
Hearst, William Randolph, 37, 75, 81, 82, 83, 86, 102, 107, 144
Hearst's Magazine, 128, 141
Hendricks, Burton J., 95
Henry, O., 144-45
Herbert, Victor, 121
Herrick, Robert, 110
Hill, James S., 162
Hillis, Mrs. Newell Dwight, 103, 105, 106
The History of Great American Fortunes, 83
Hobbes, Thomas, 153
Hodder, Alfred, 143-44
The House of Bondage, 147-48
The House of Mirth, 44
Hoyt, Eleanor, 50
Hubbard, Elbert, 103, 124, 162, 163-64
Hughes, Charles Evans, 86
Hugo, Victor, 17
Hunter, Robert, 59
Hyde, James Hazen, 96

Independent, 94, 96, 137

Jackson, Gabrielle E., 101
James, Henry, 105, 110
Janvier, Thomas A., 56
Johnson, Tom, 49
The Jungle, 144
Juvenal, 116, 163

Kauffman, Reginald Wright, 147-48
Kemble, E. W., 86
Kipling, Rudyard, 89
Knox, Philander Chase, 85

Index

818.52
R256

DATE DUE

GAYLORD			PRINTED IN U.S.A.